Bron Yr Aur through time and seasons

Hidden in the hills surrounding Machynlleth, Snowdonia, I have whiled away hours, days and years. In all life's changes I have felt the same slate beneath my feet, heard the same latch on the door, and breathed the same unique combination of bracken, stone and sea-air from the West. And now these stones and trees that have themselves heard and seen so much, have their essence caught not only in music,but in paint, carving and print, and it is my privilege to be able to share a little piece of my home and heart with you. Ruth @ Bron yr aur.

Design and layout: Scott Roe
Photographs: Scott Roe, Ruth Roe & White Dove

Original 1971 slide film by kind permission of Dr Judy Dale

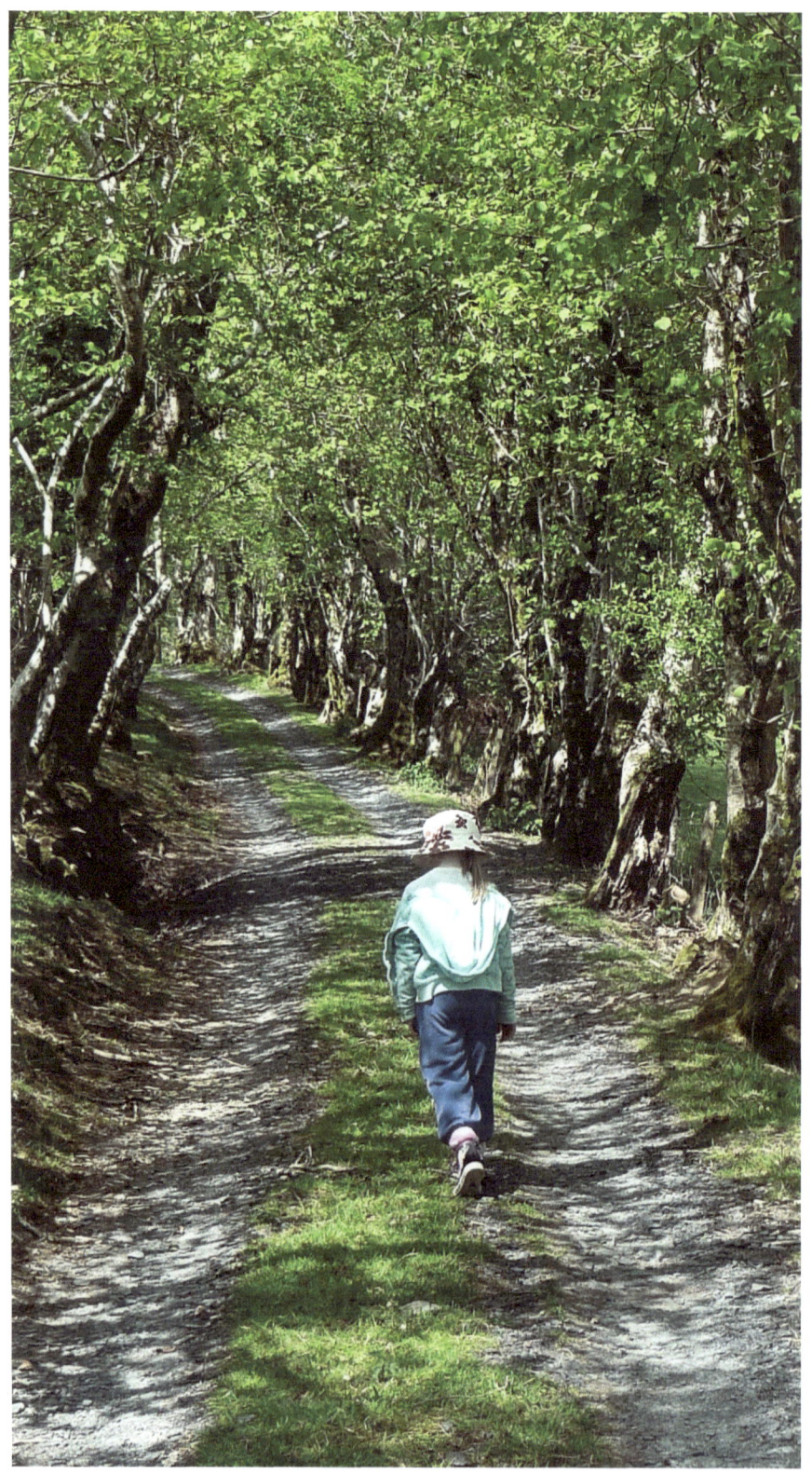

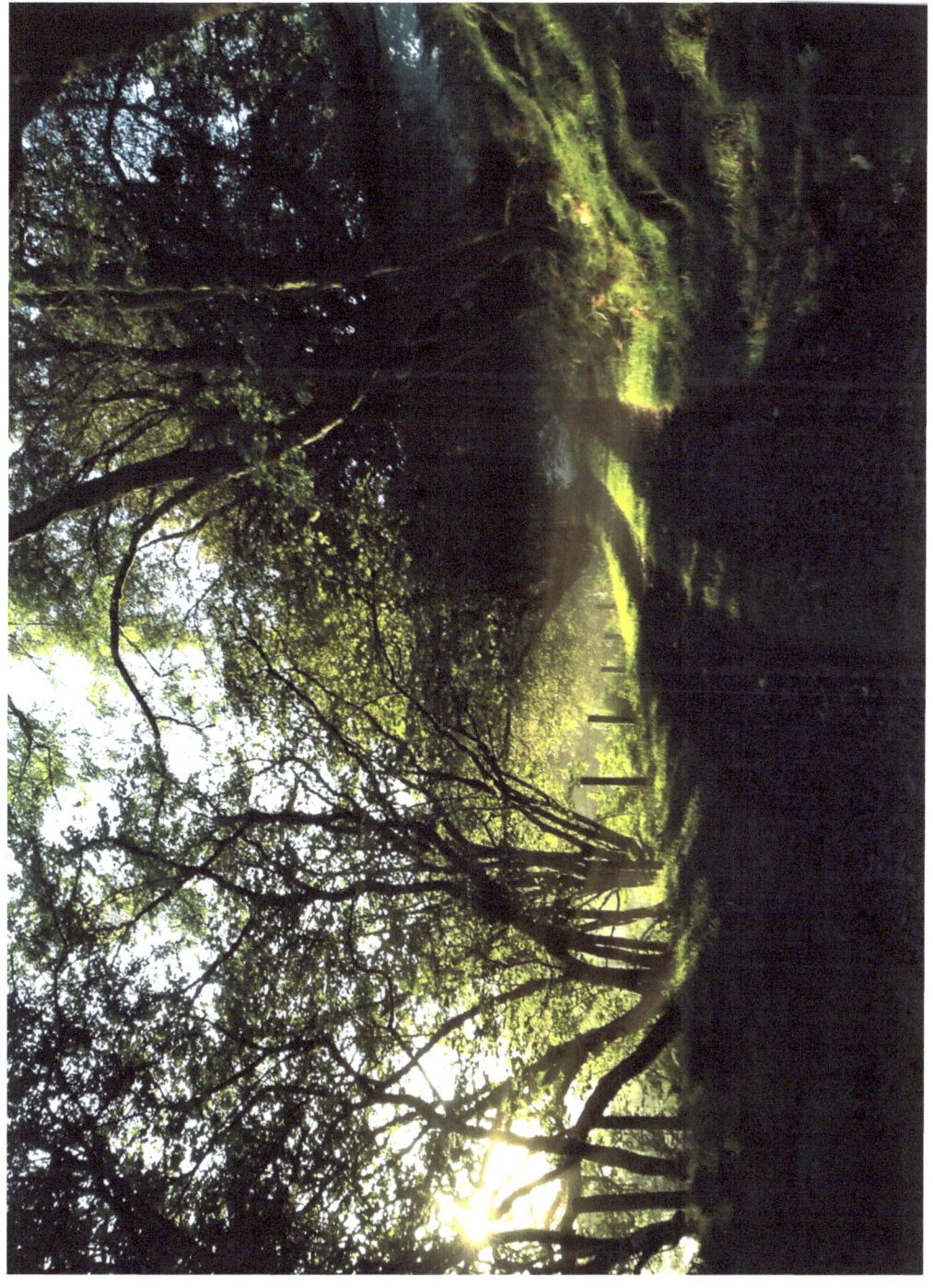

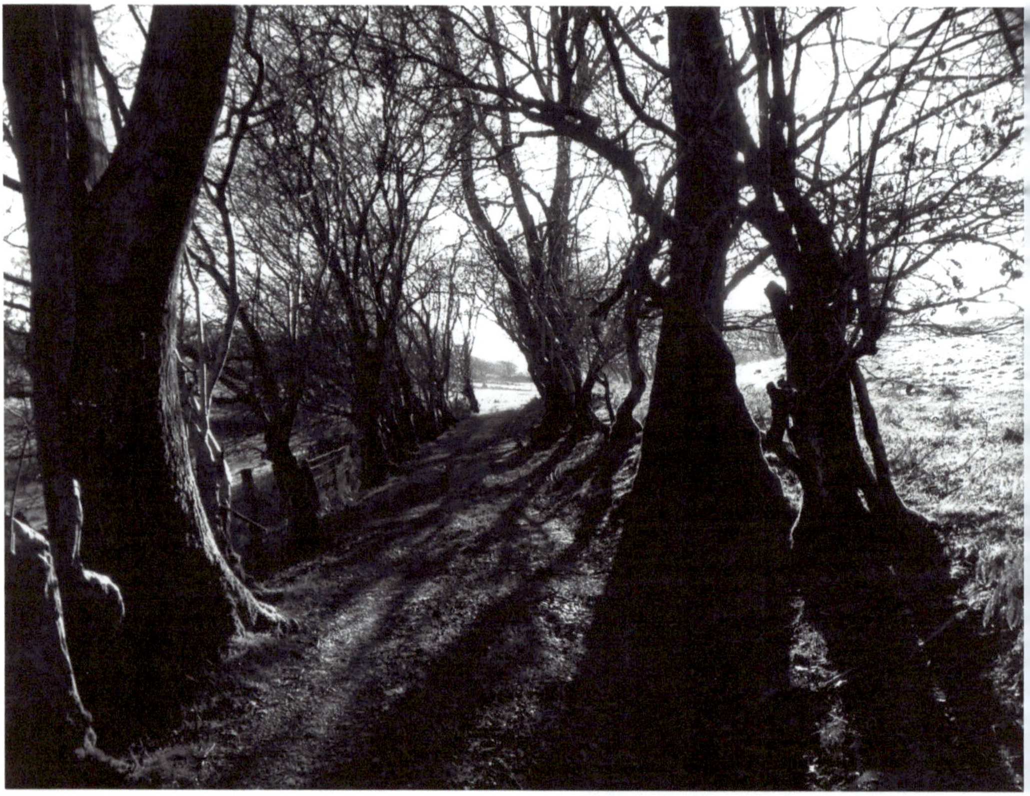

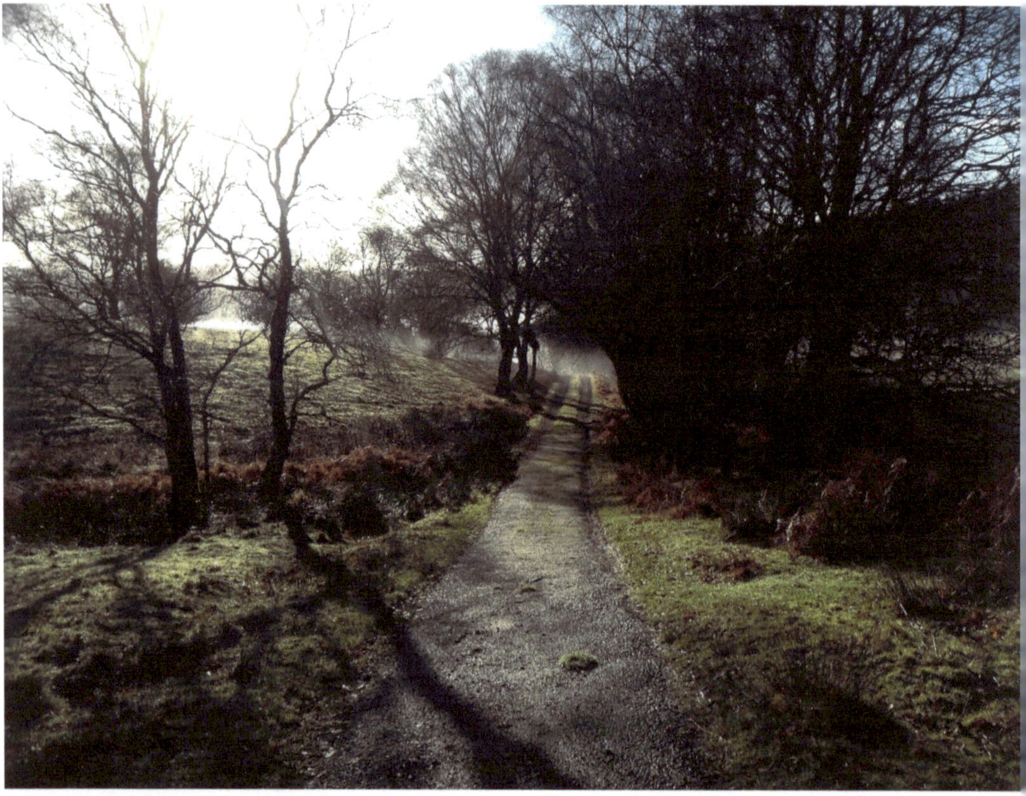

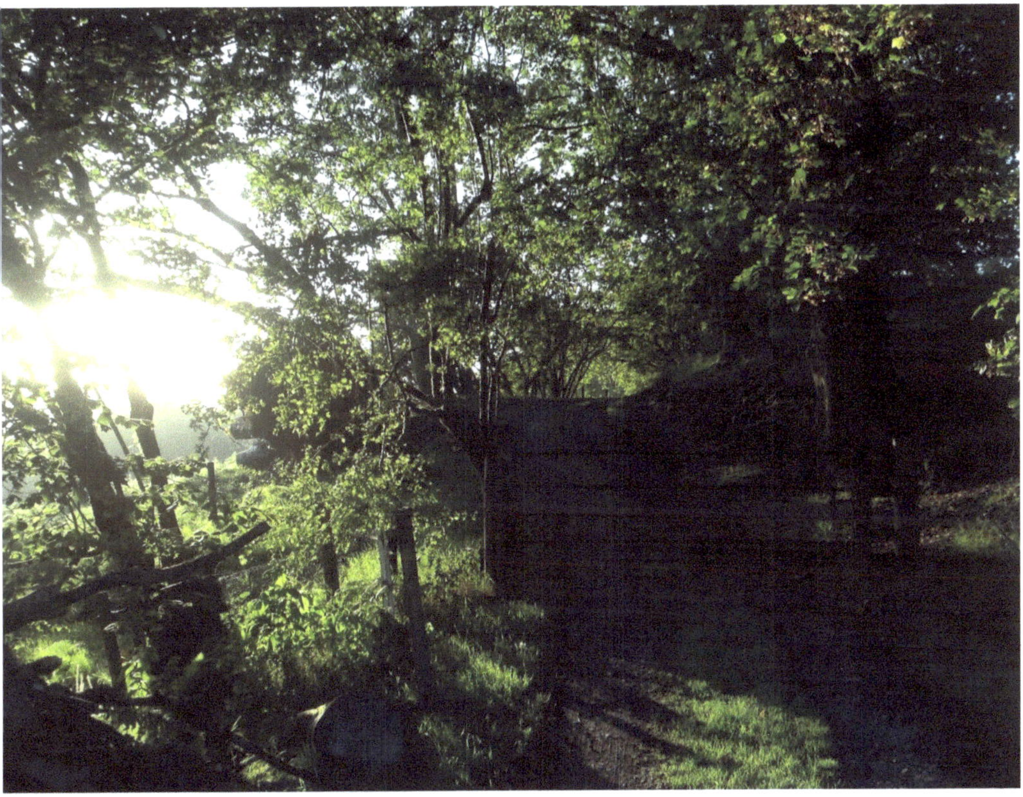

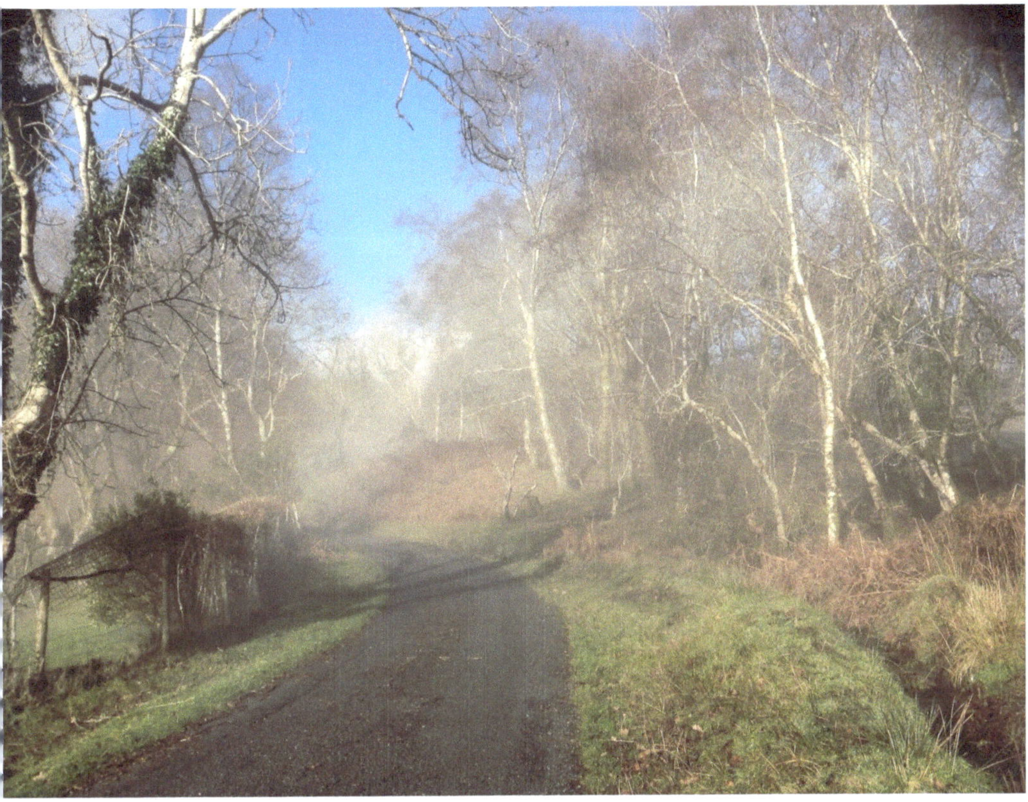

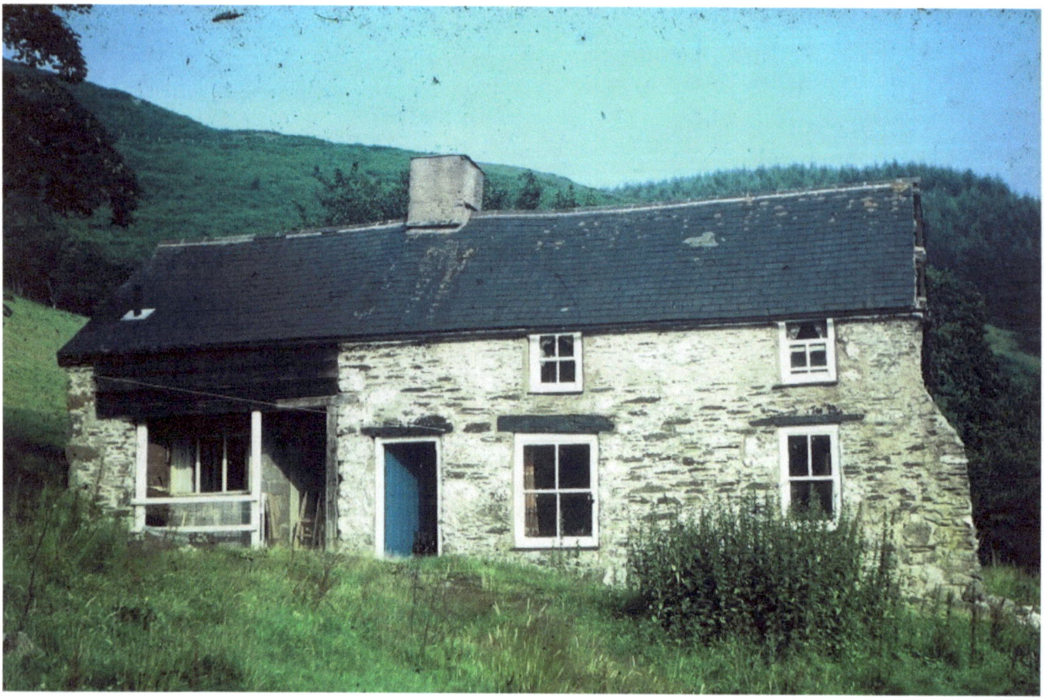

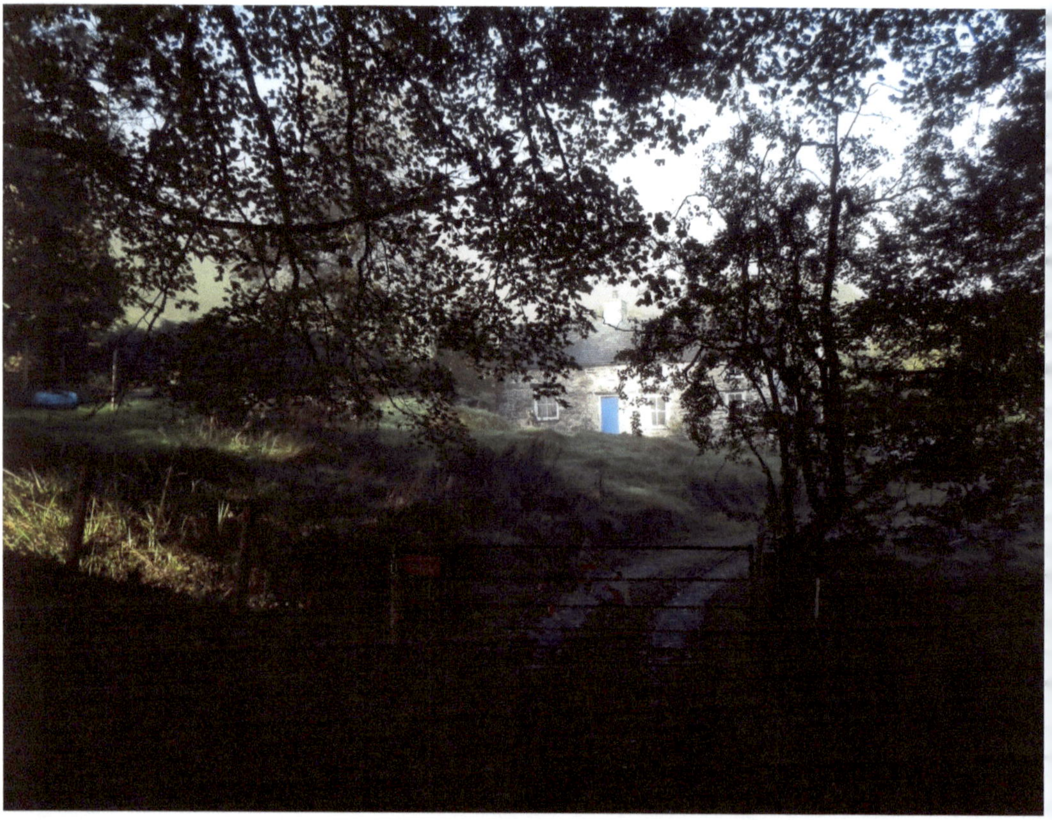

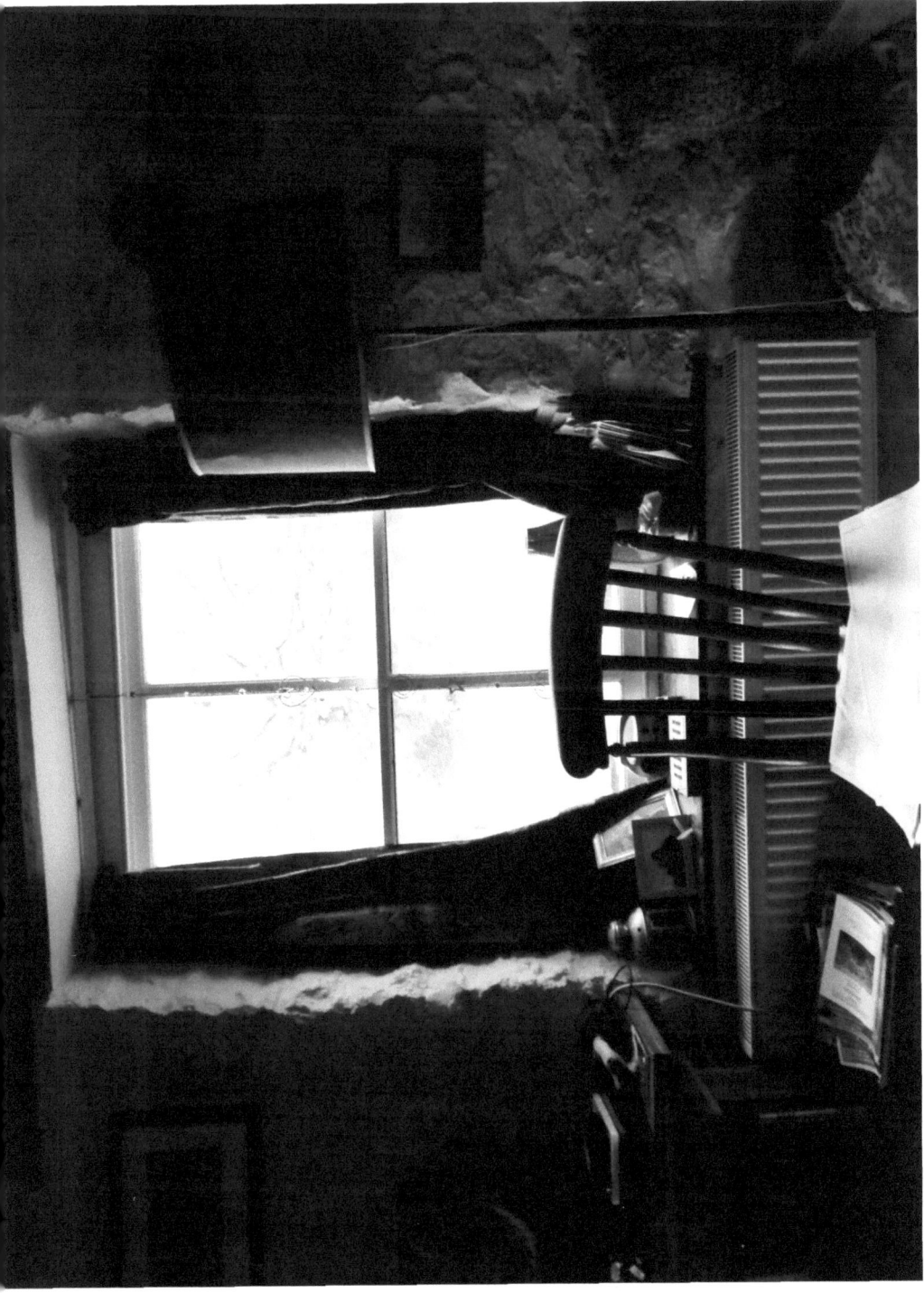

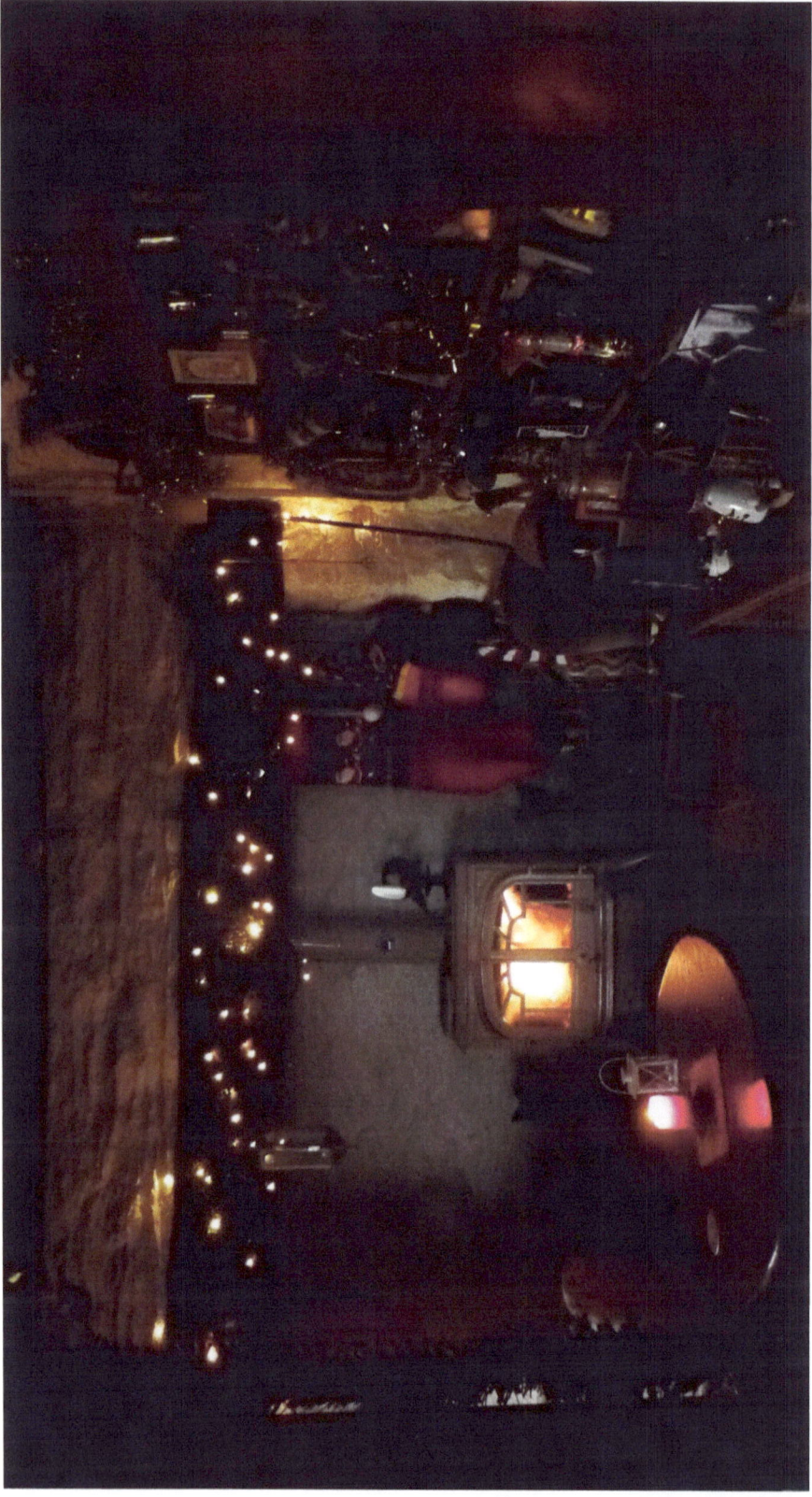

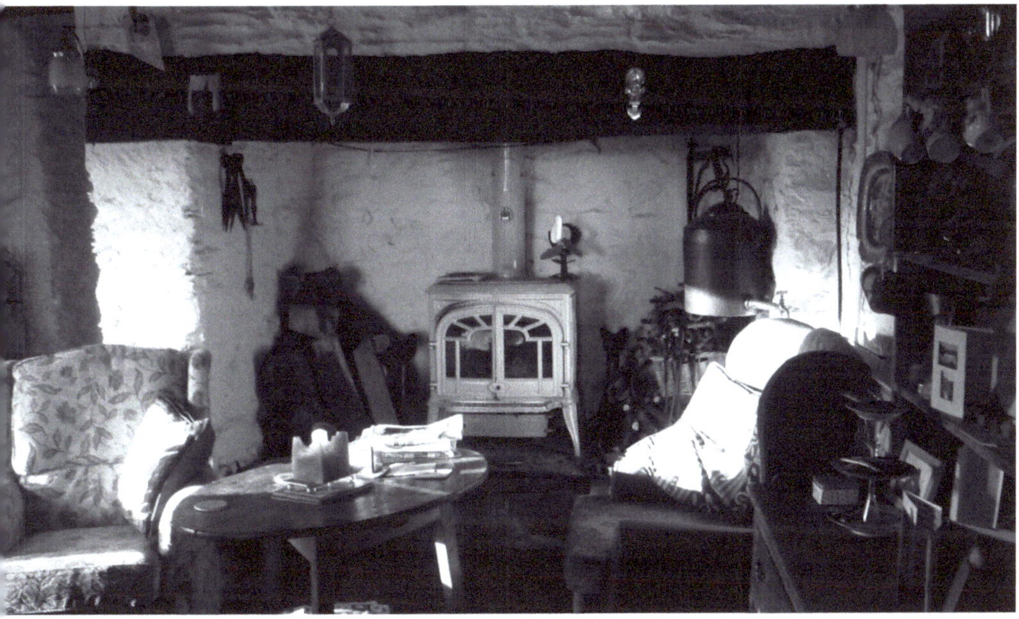

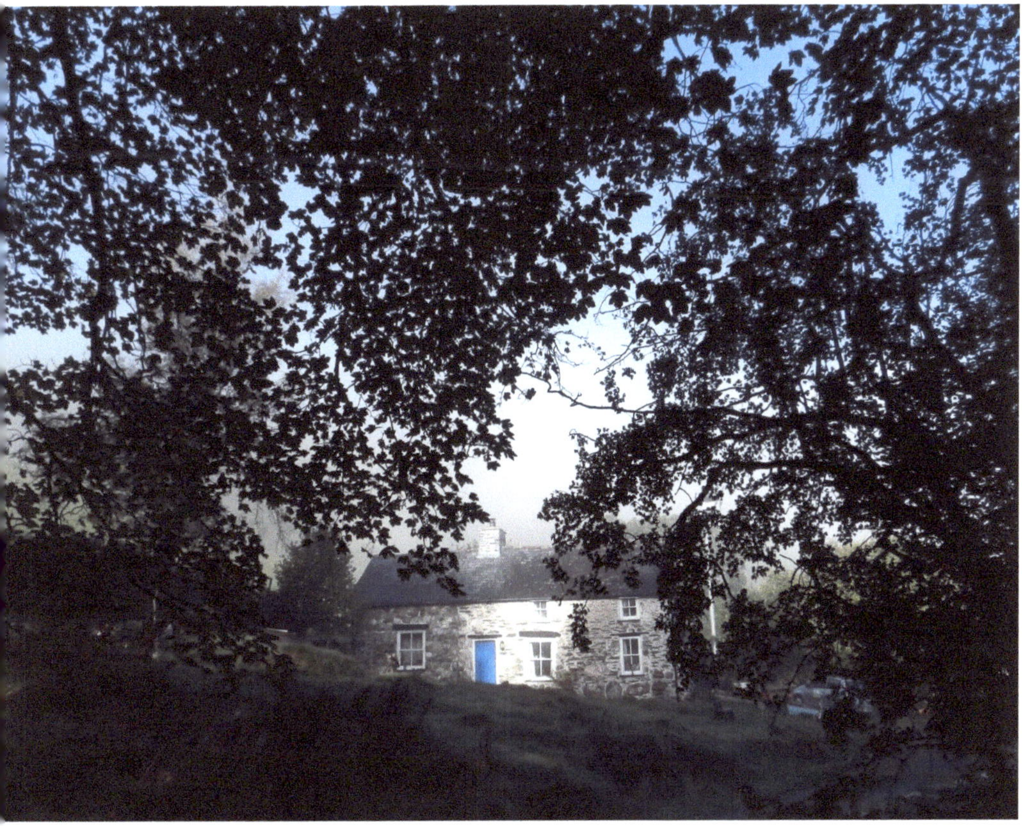

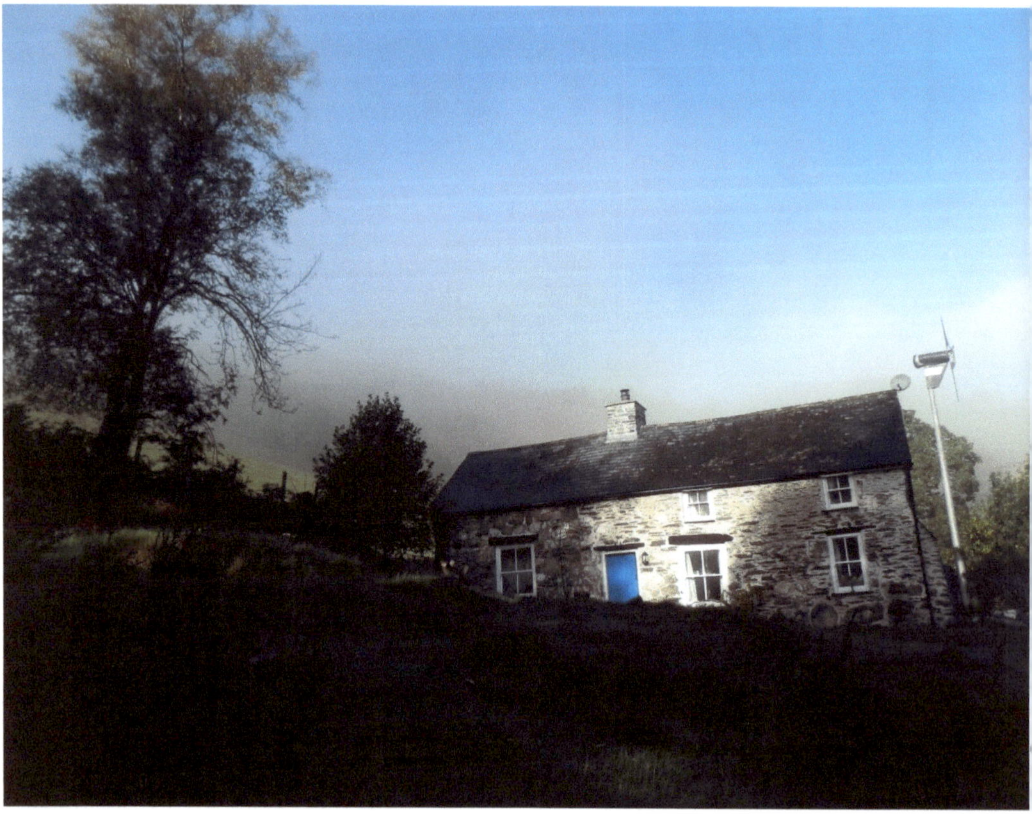

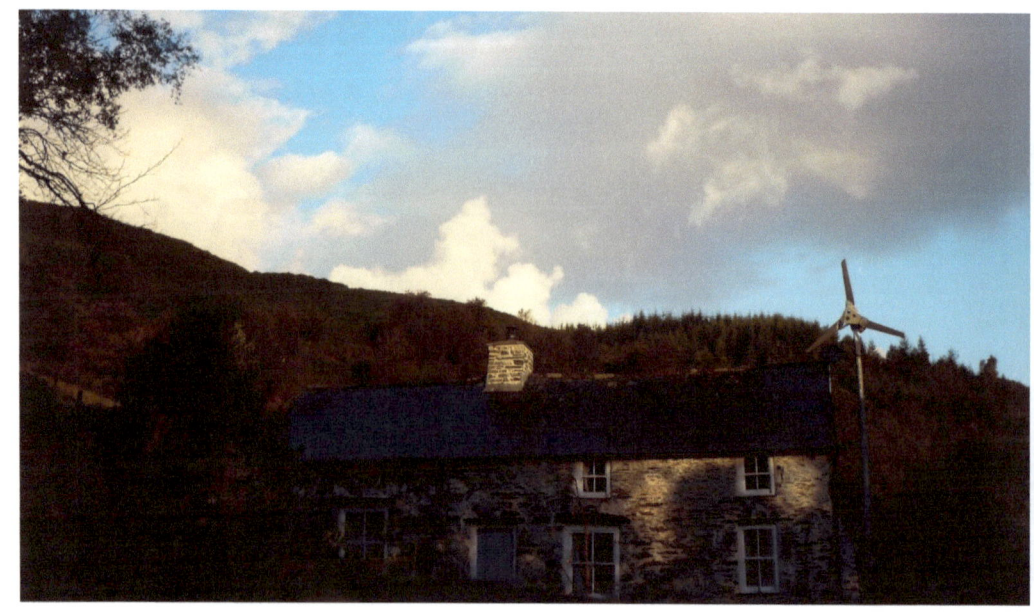

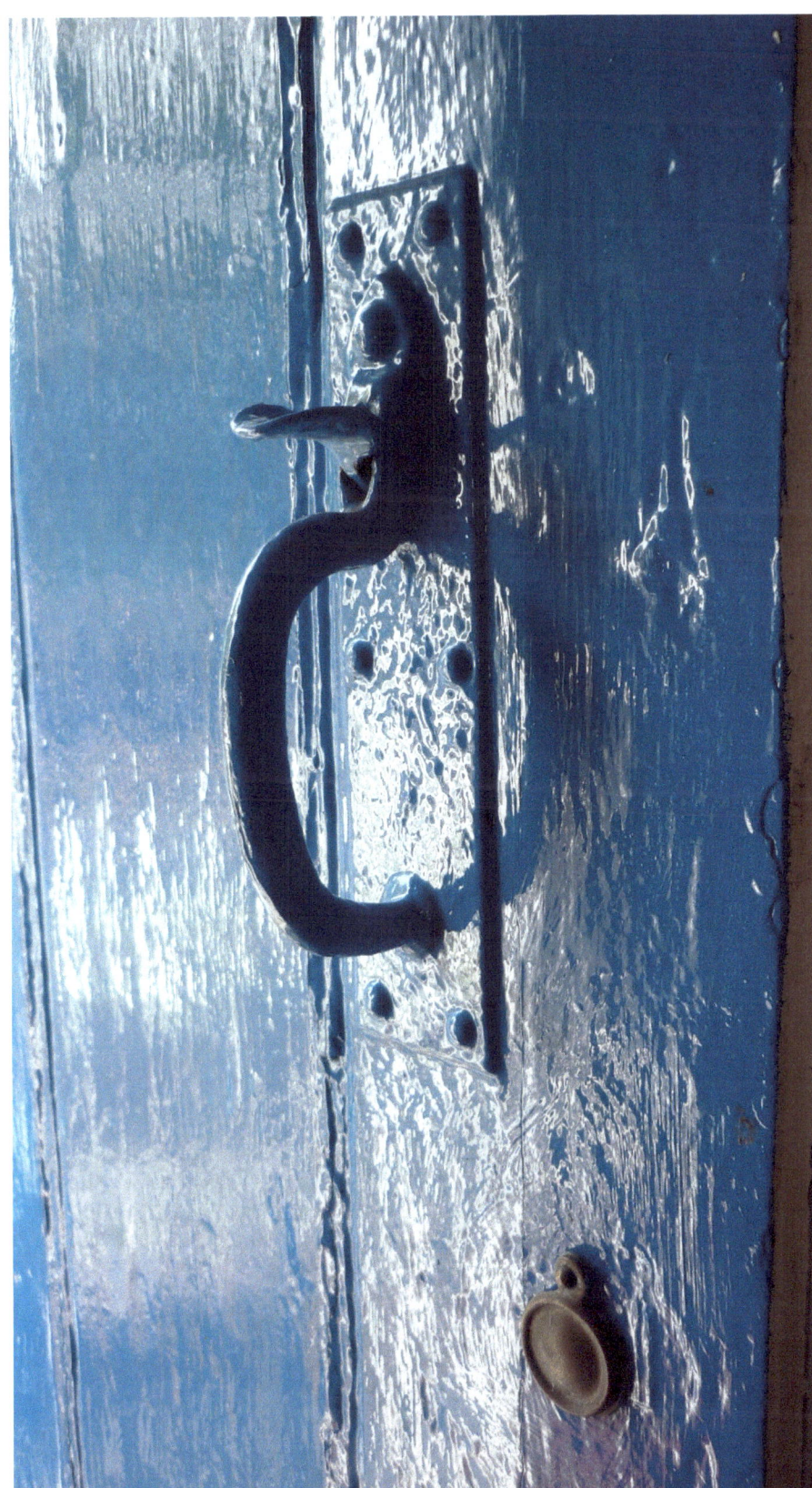

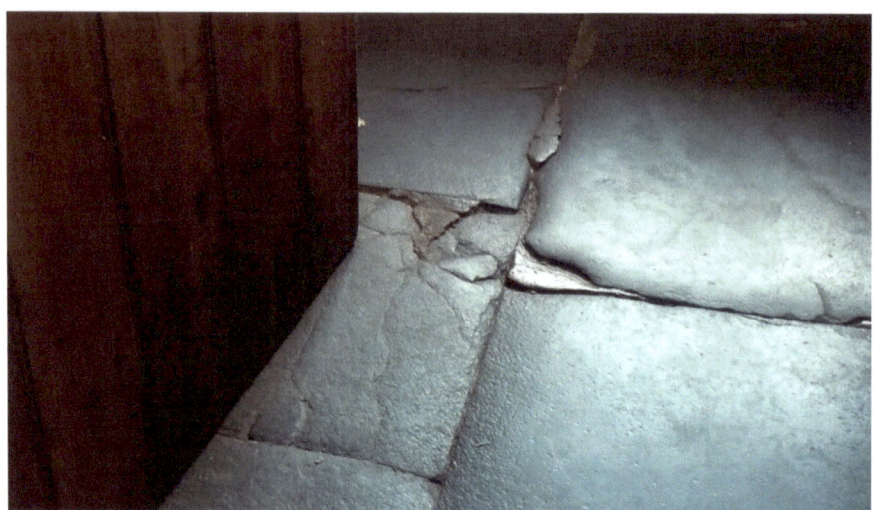

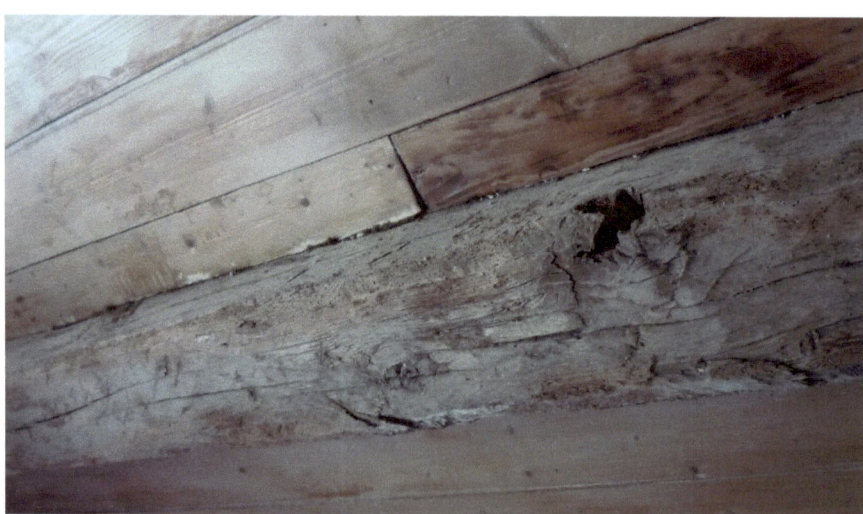

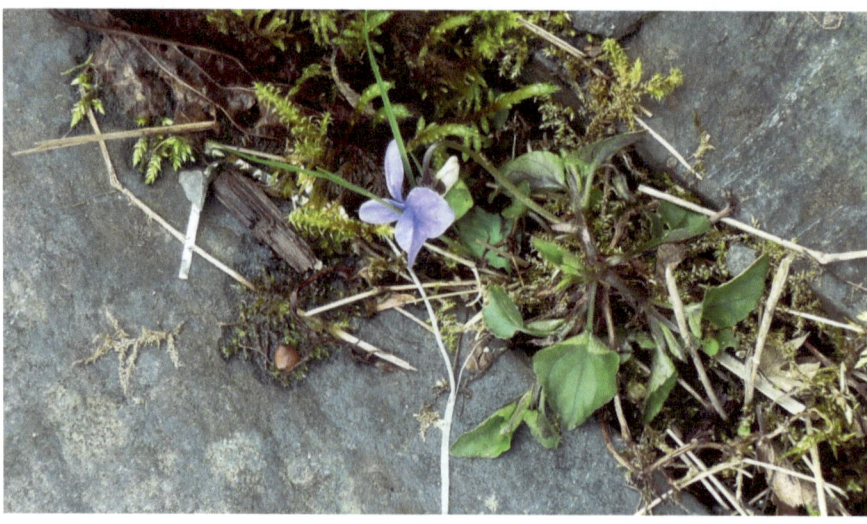

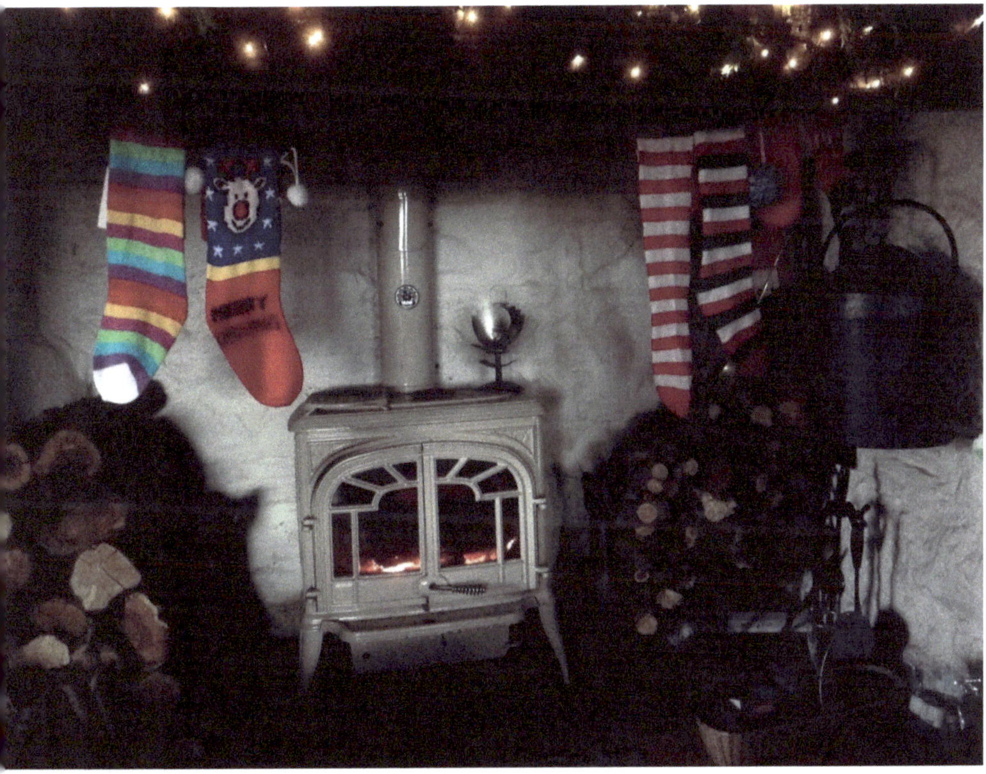

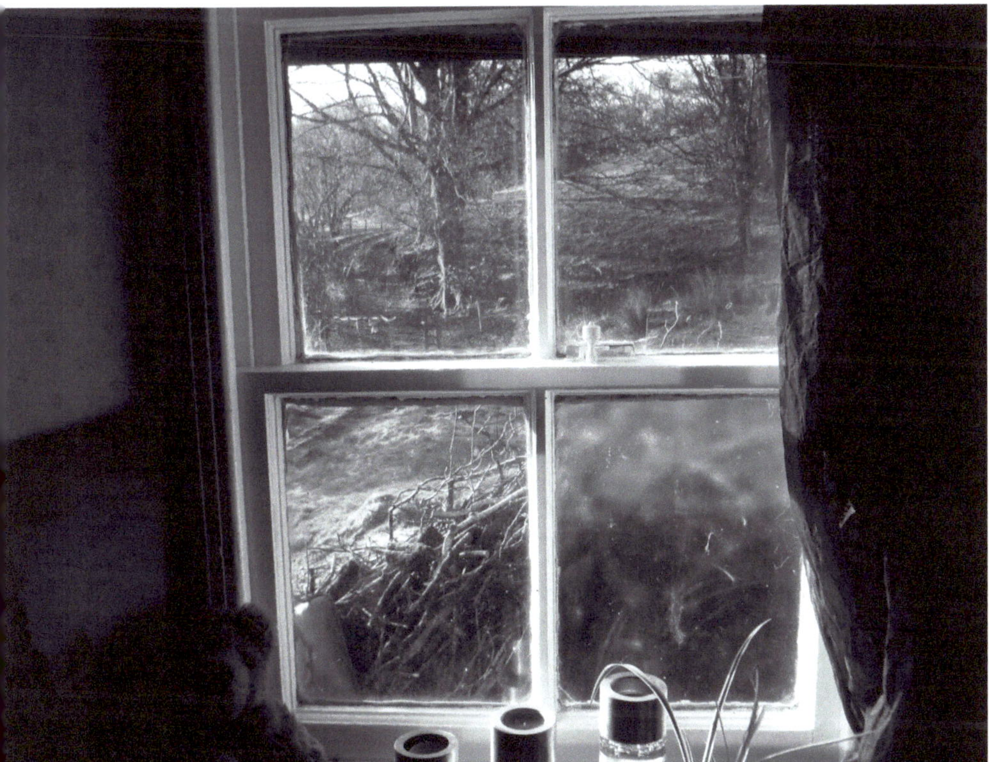

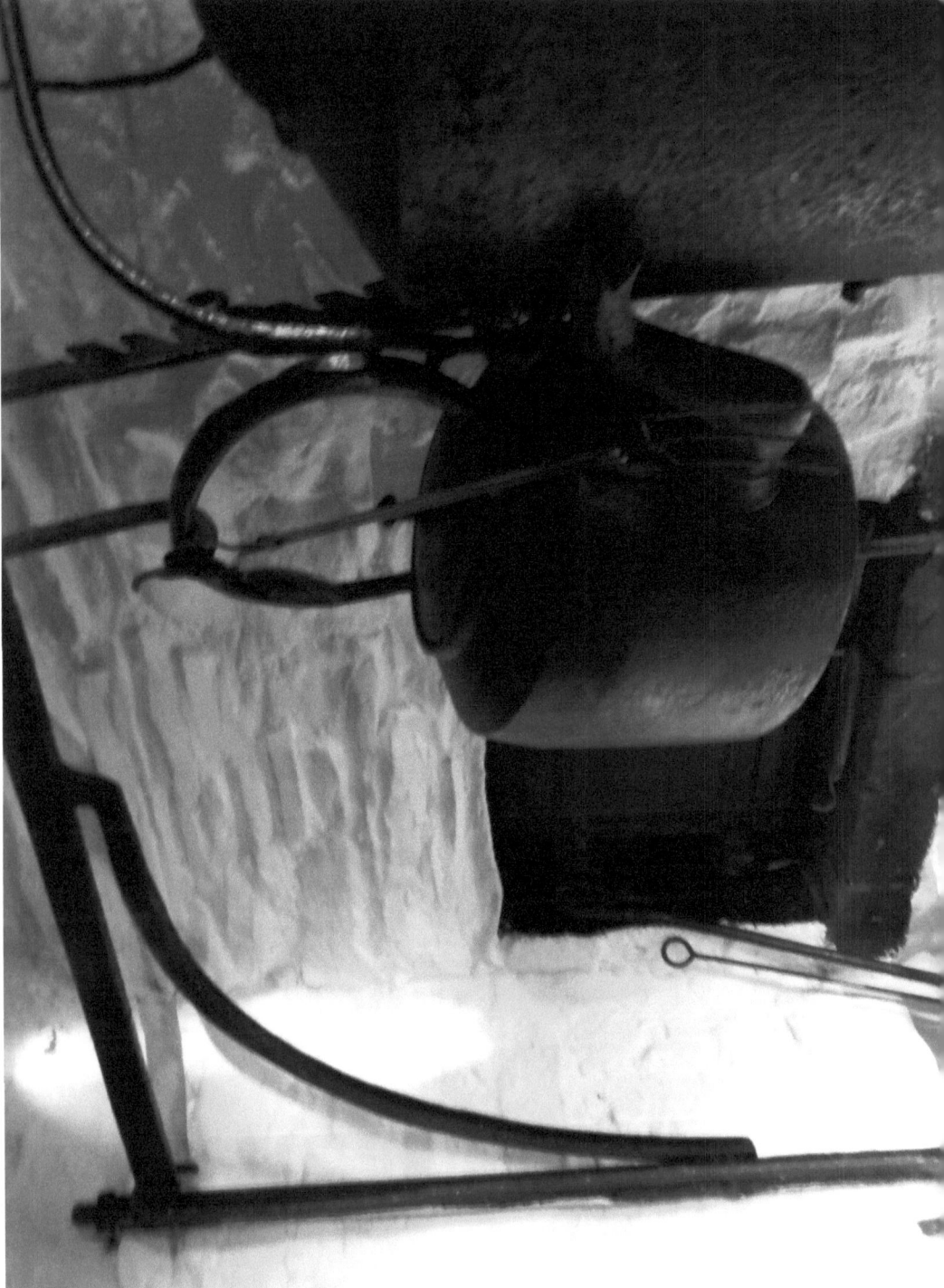

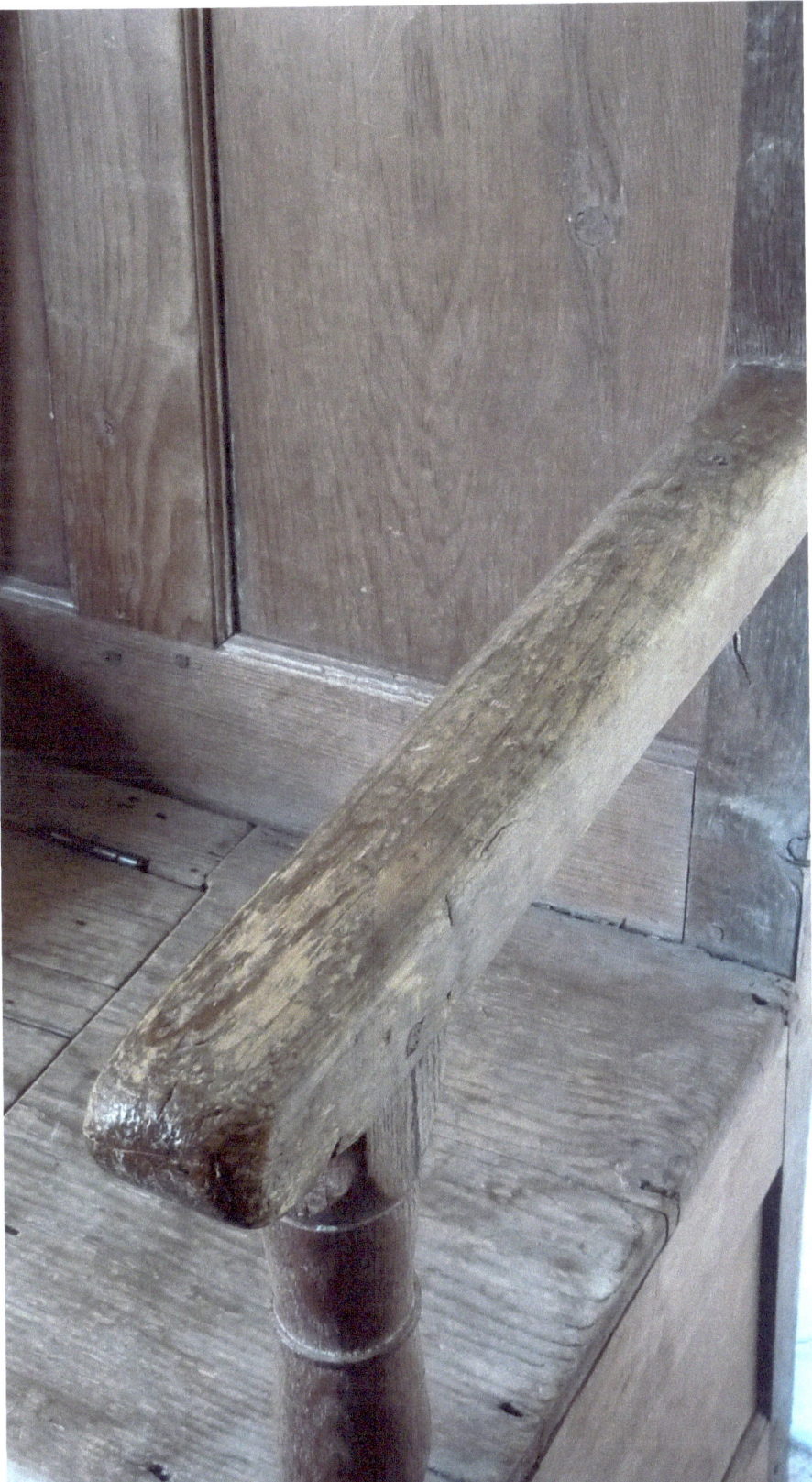

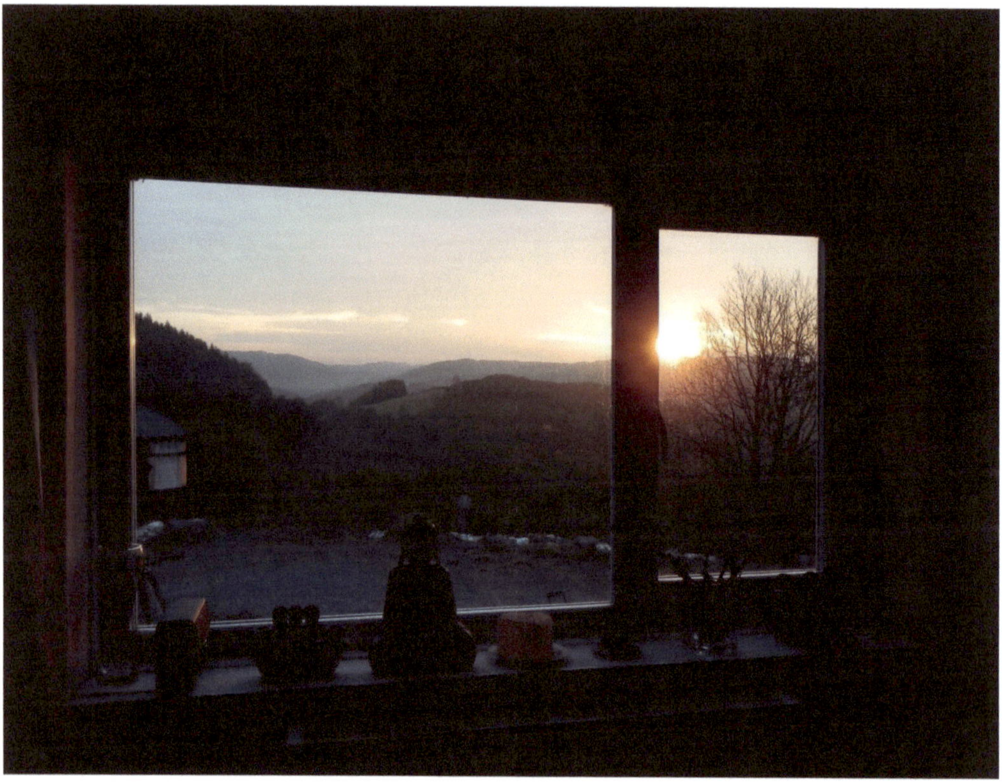

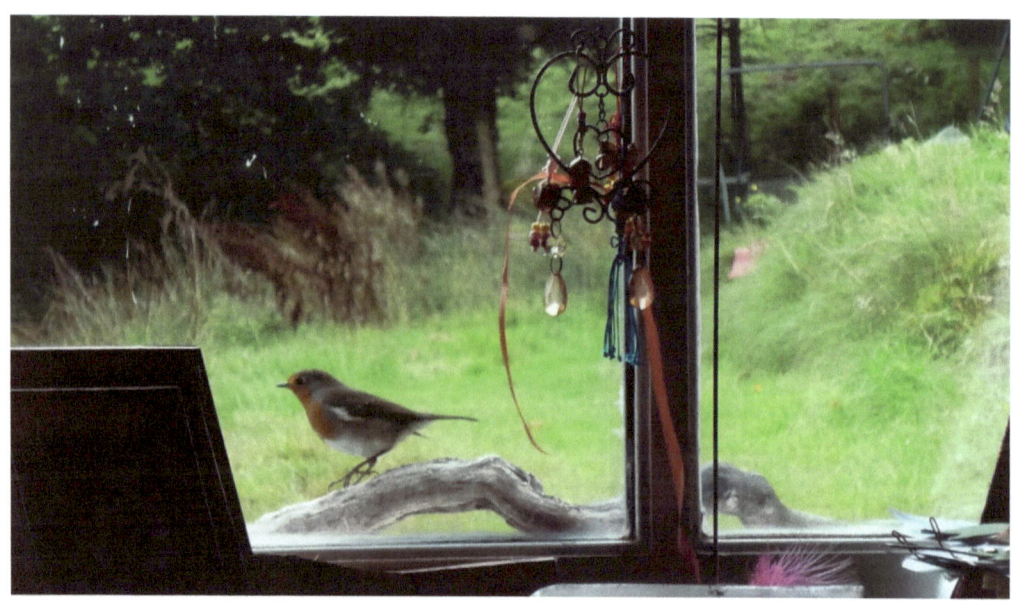

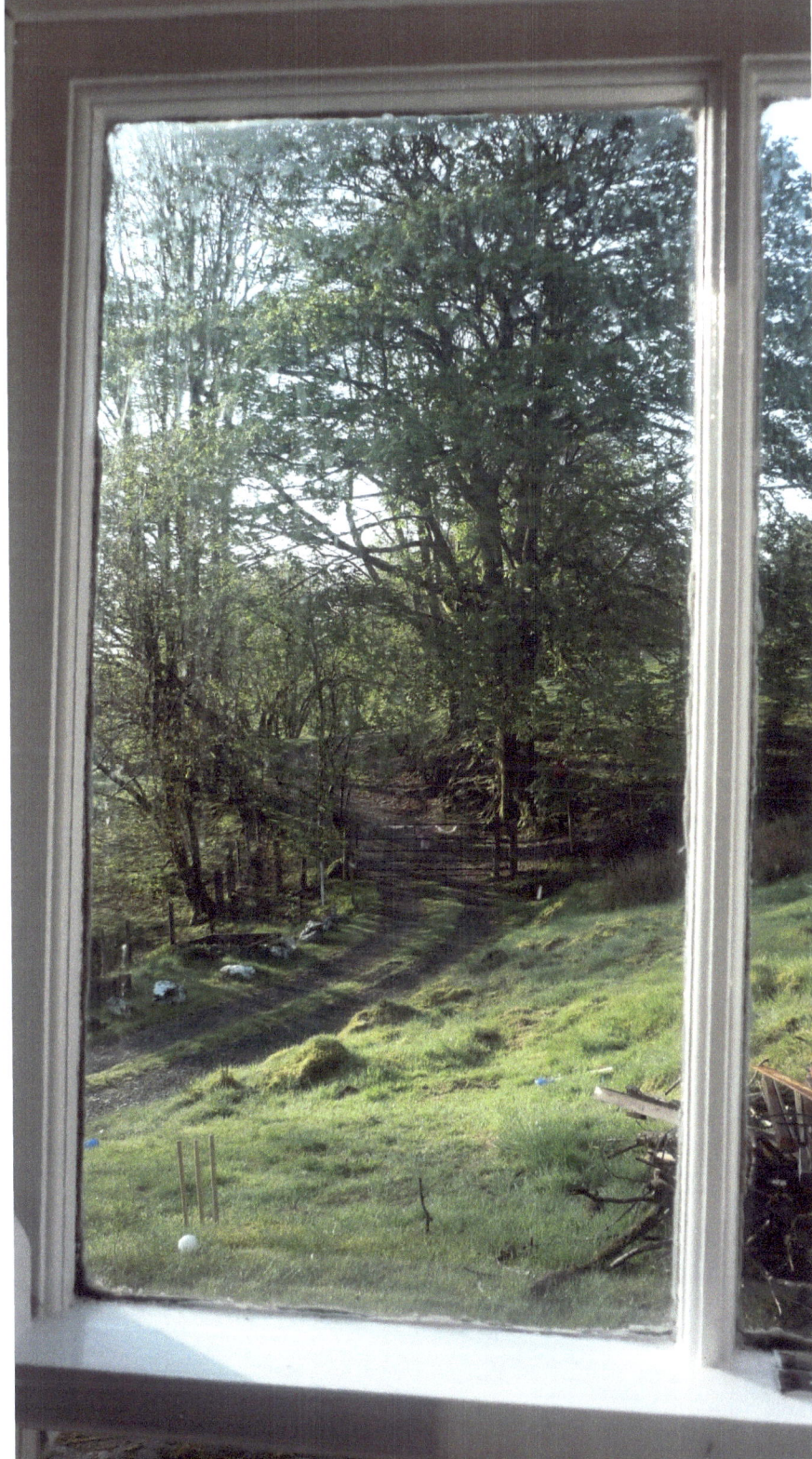

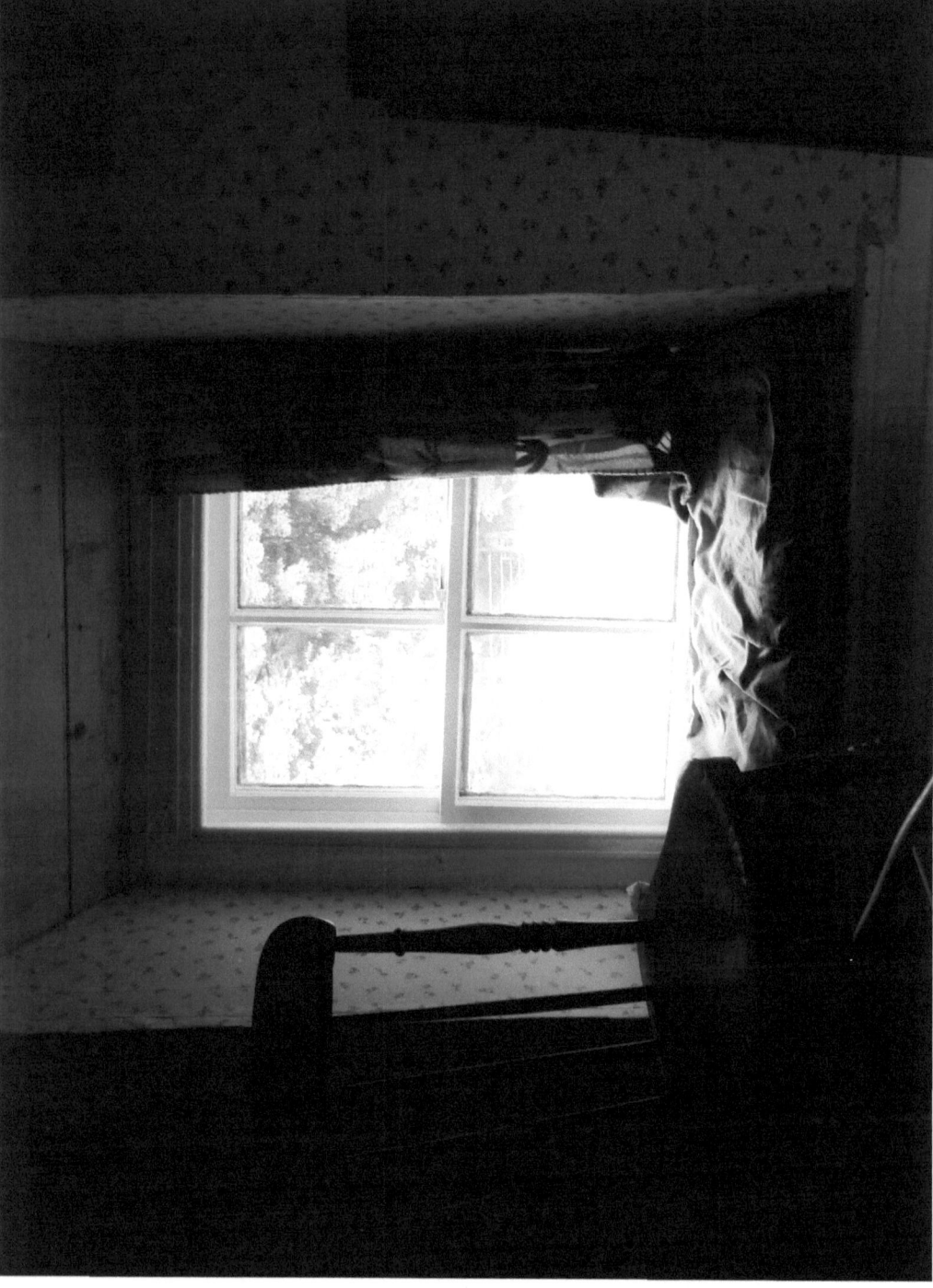

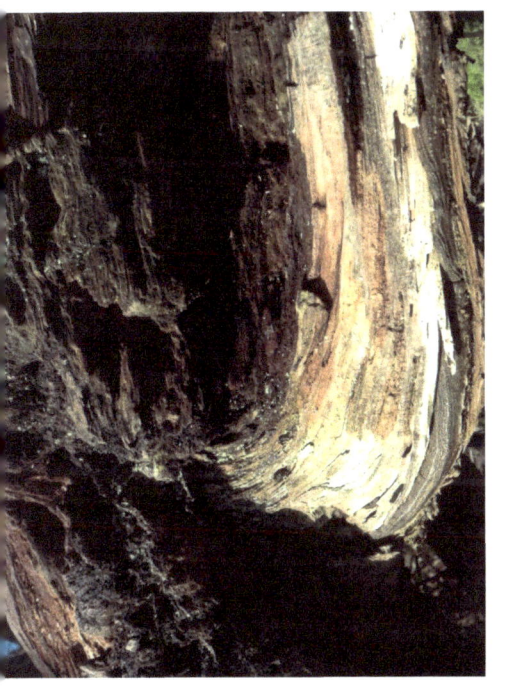
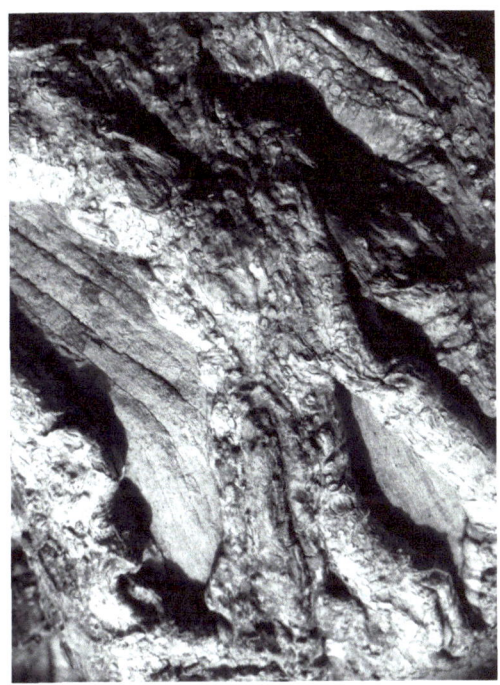
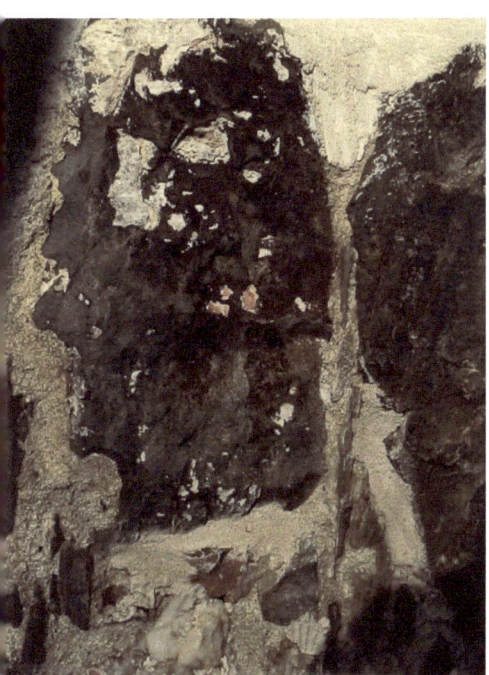
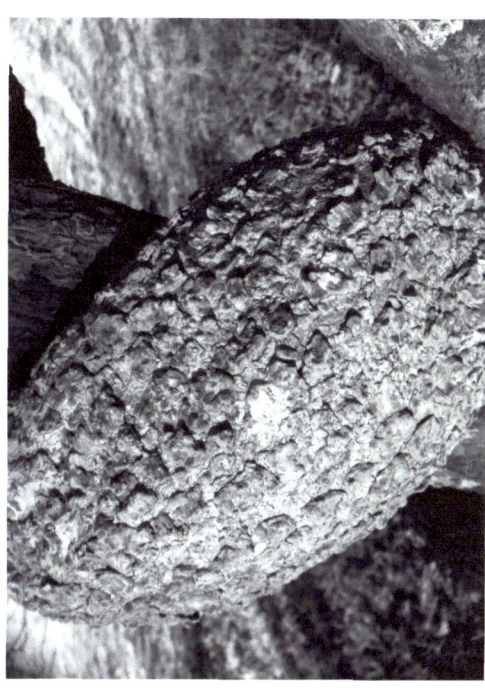

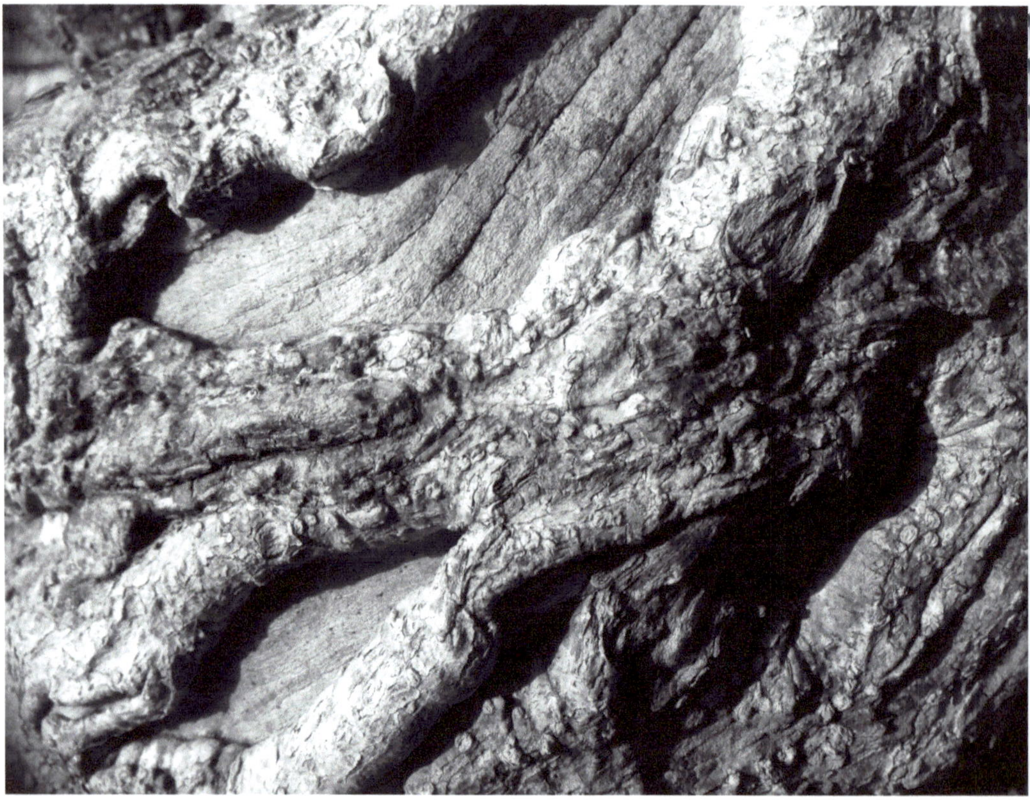

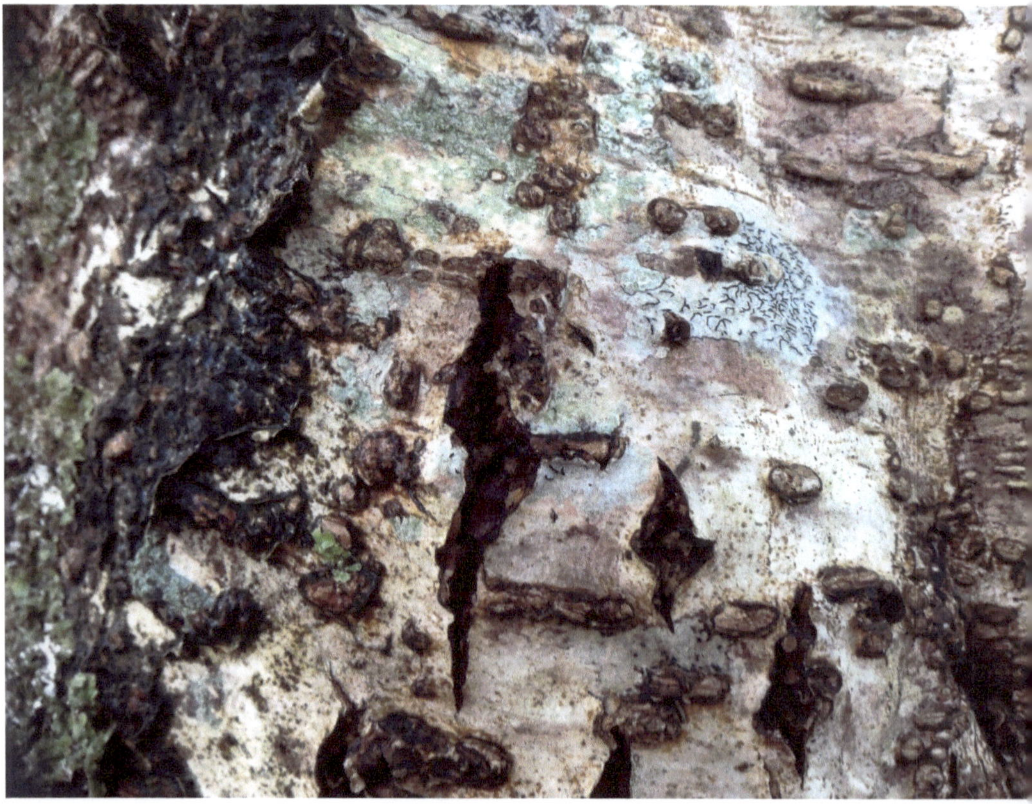

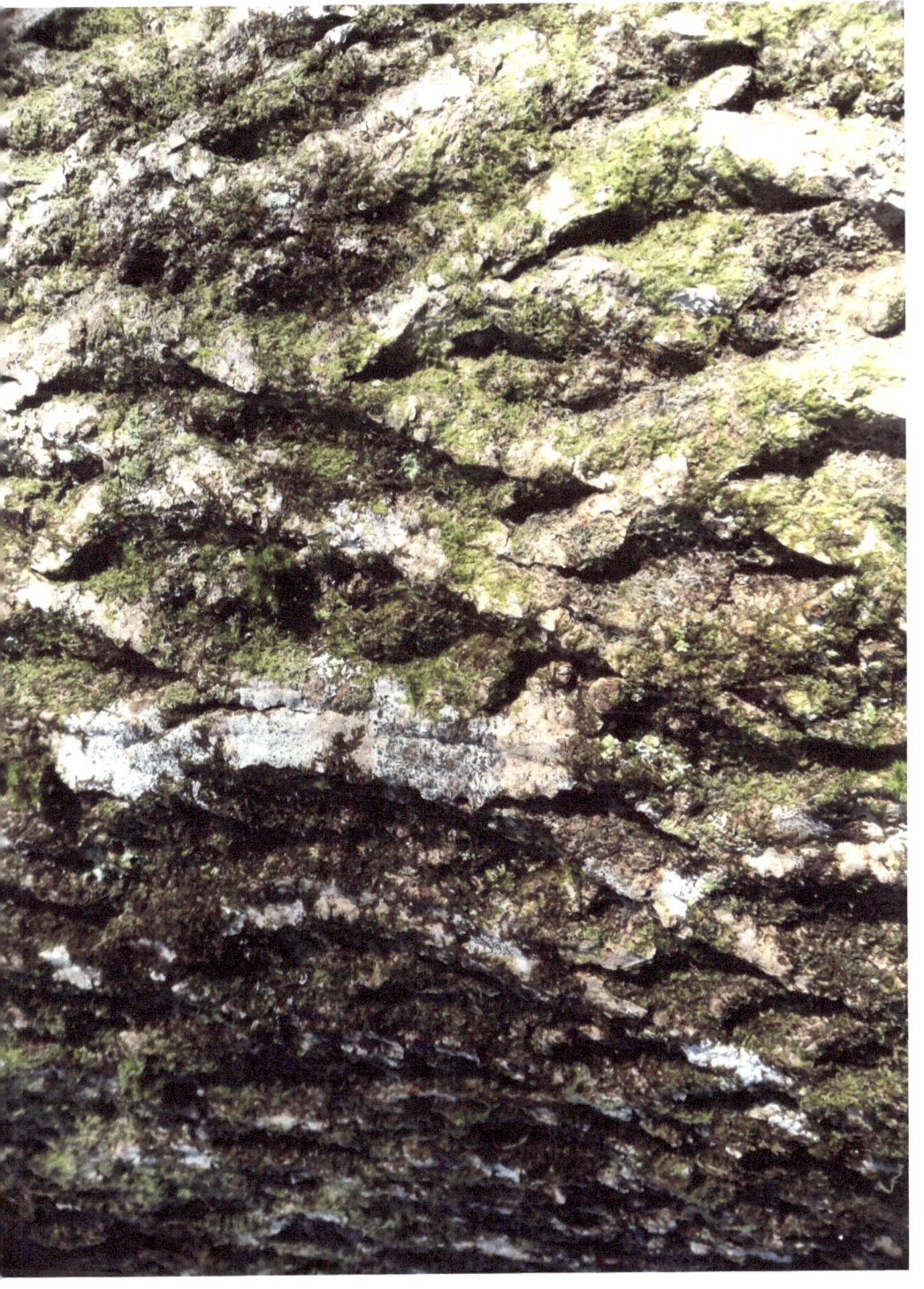

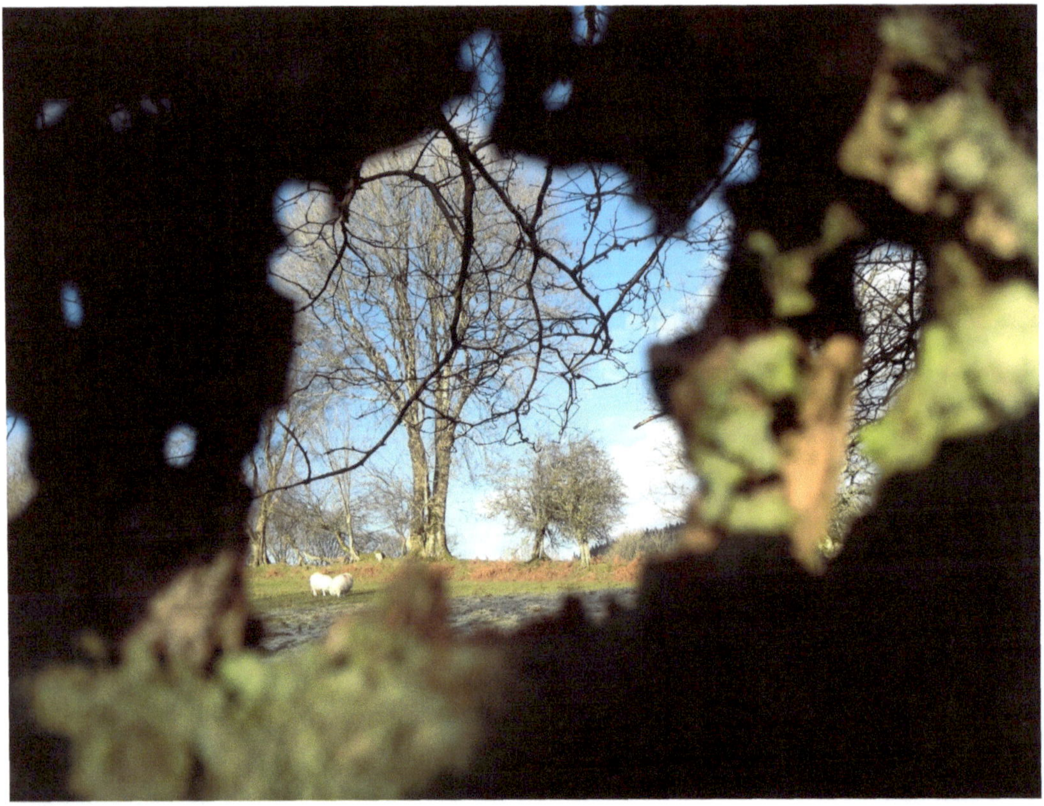

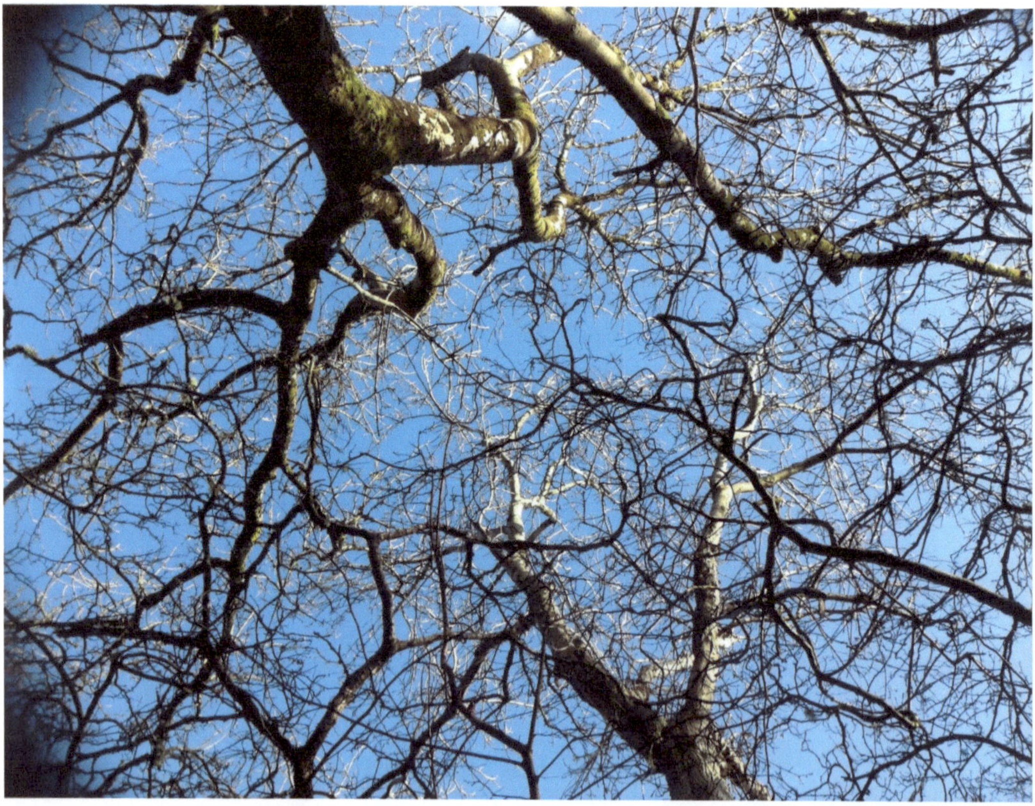

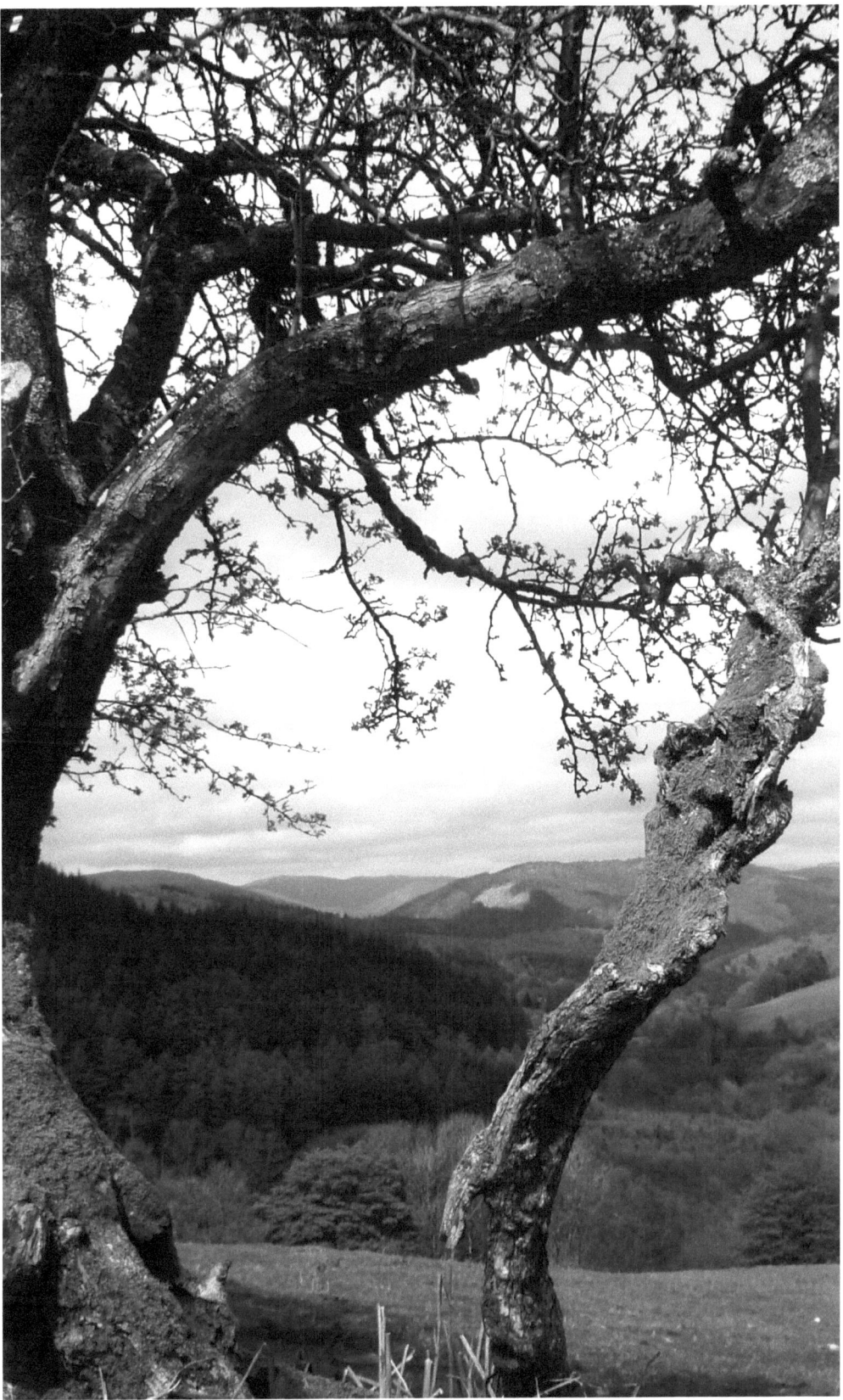

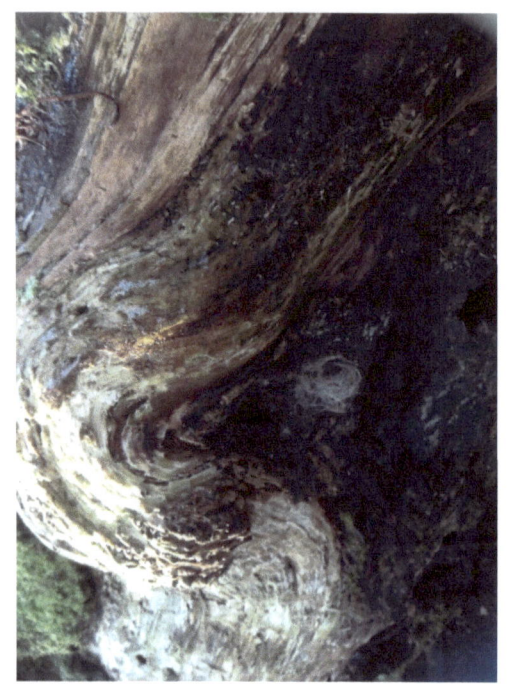
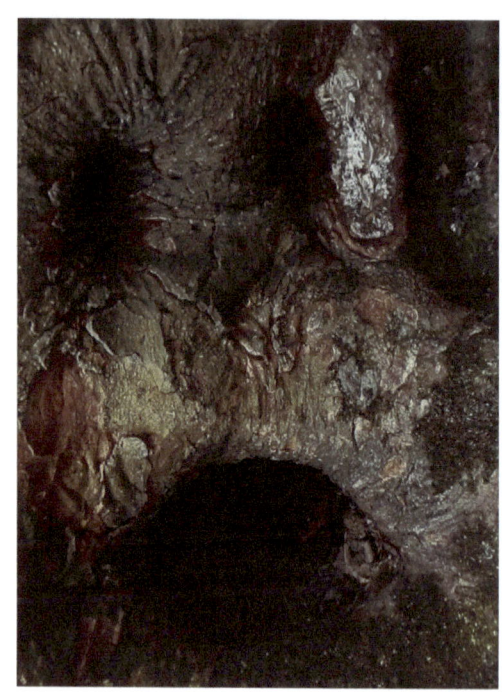
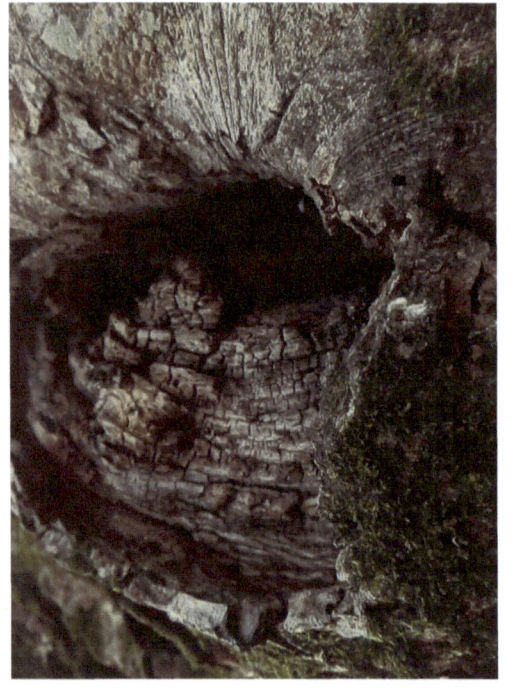
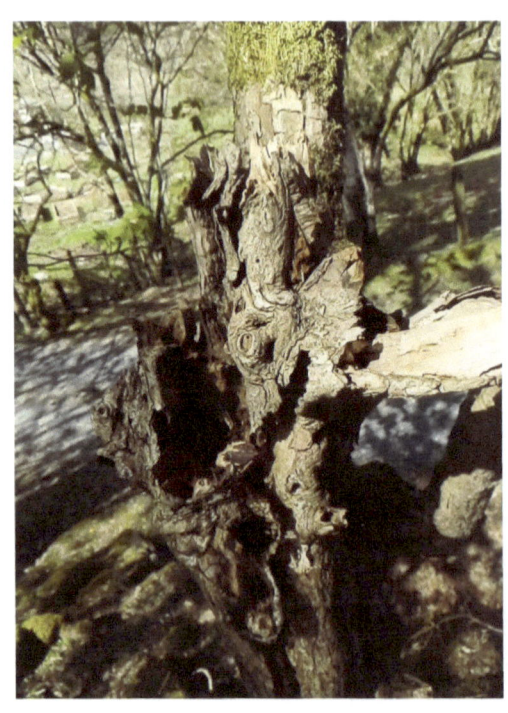

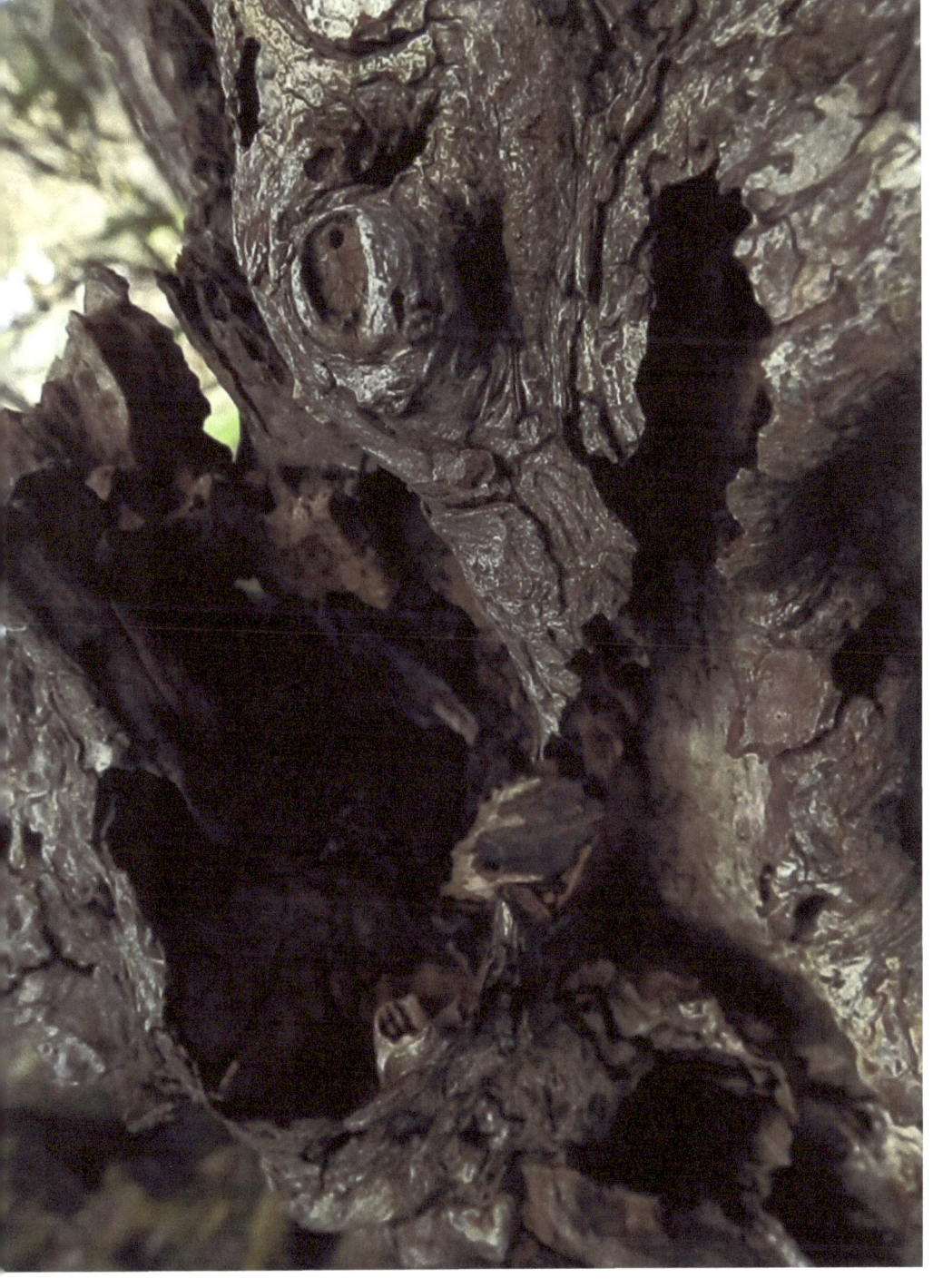

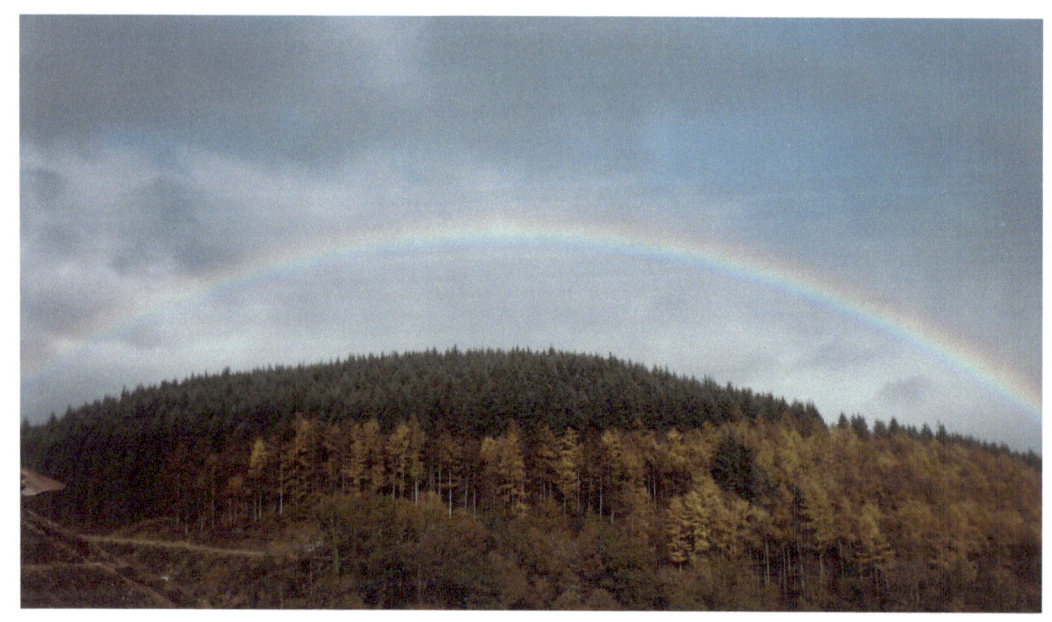

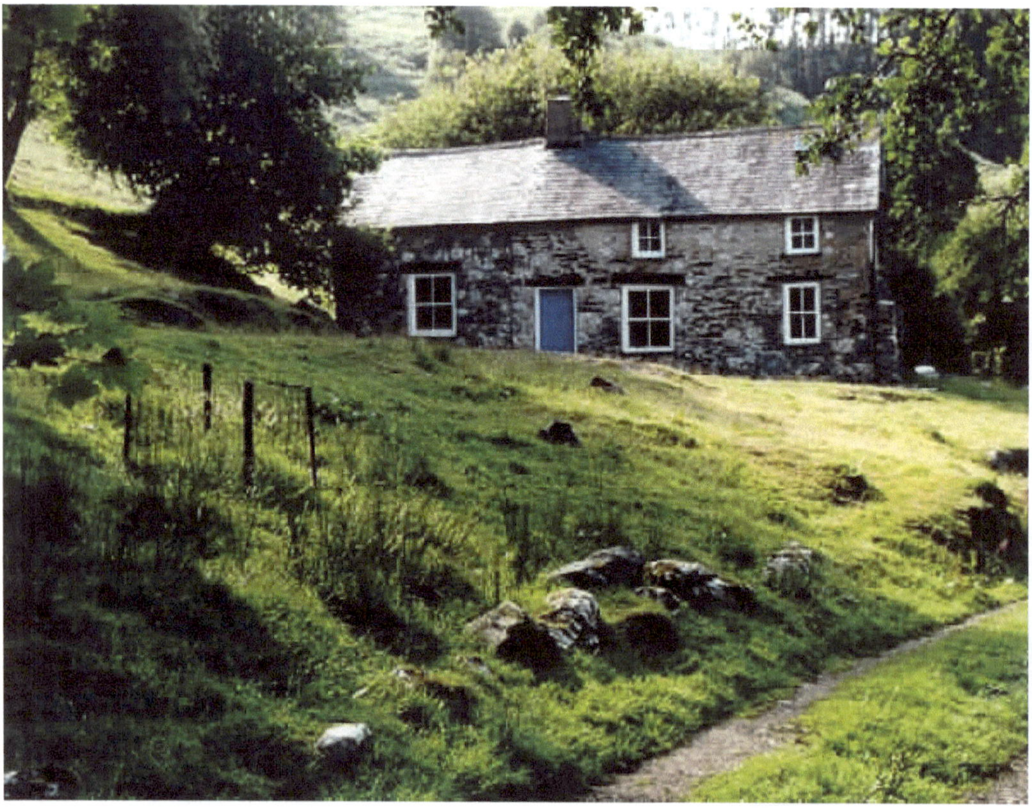

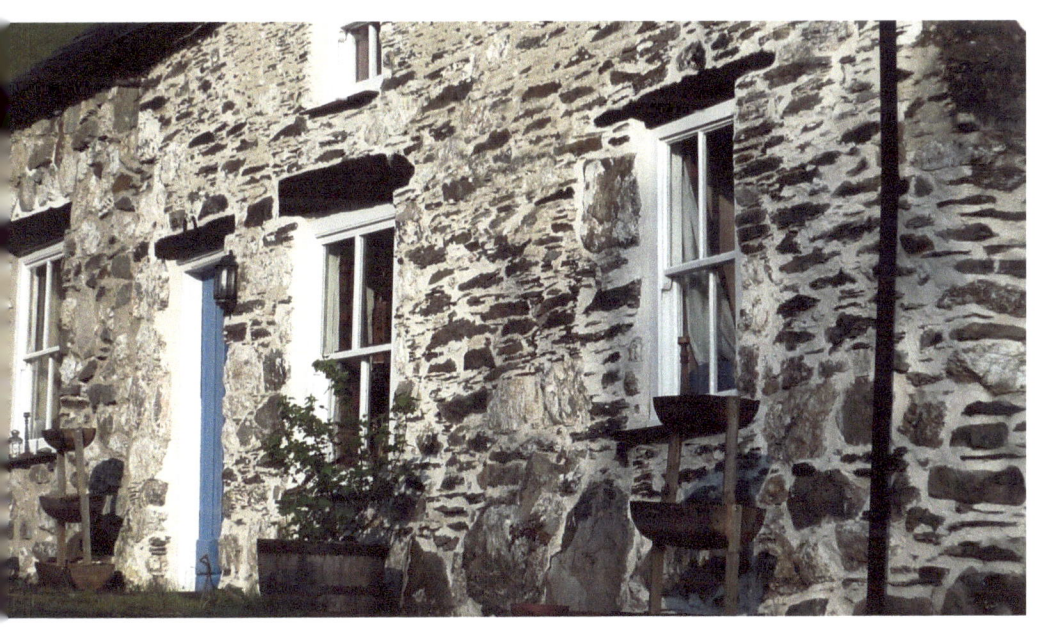

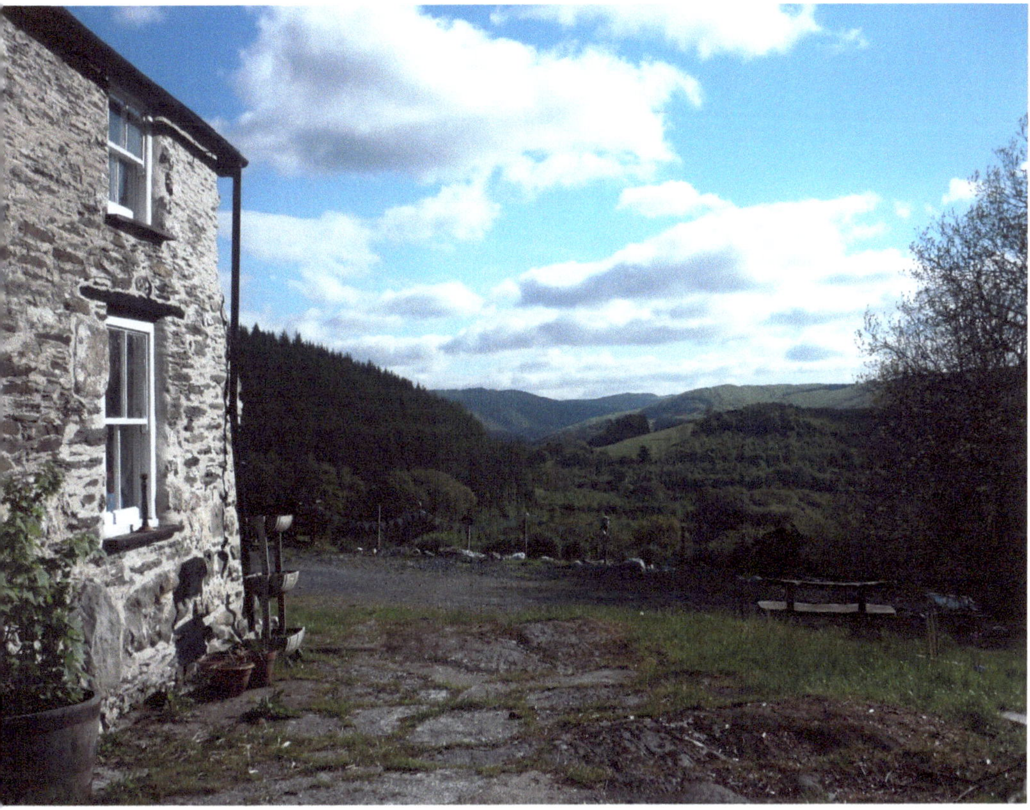

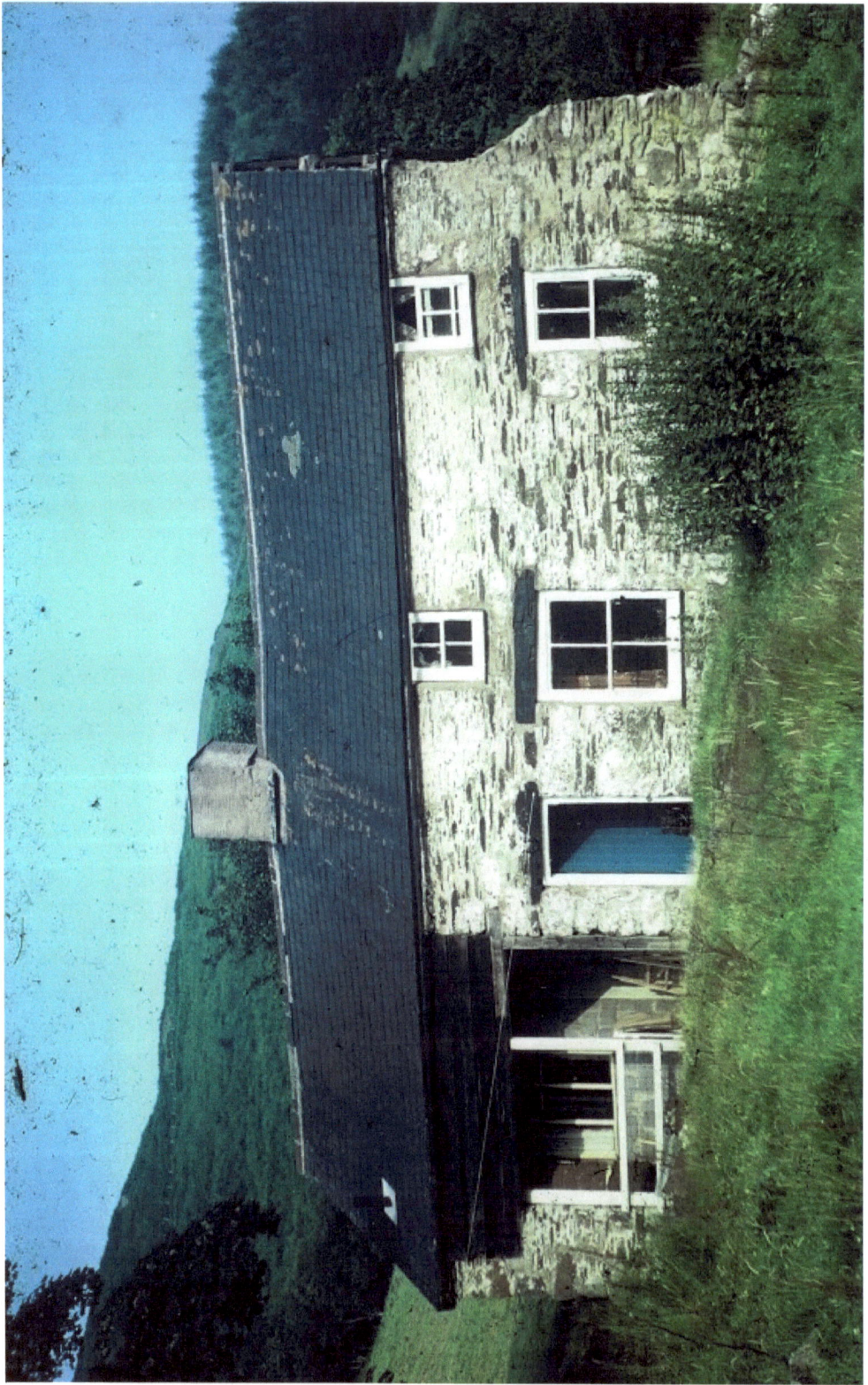

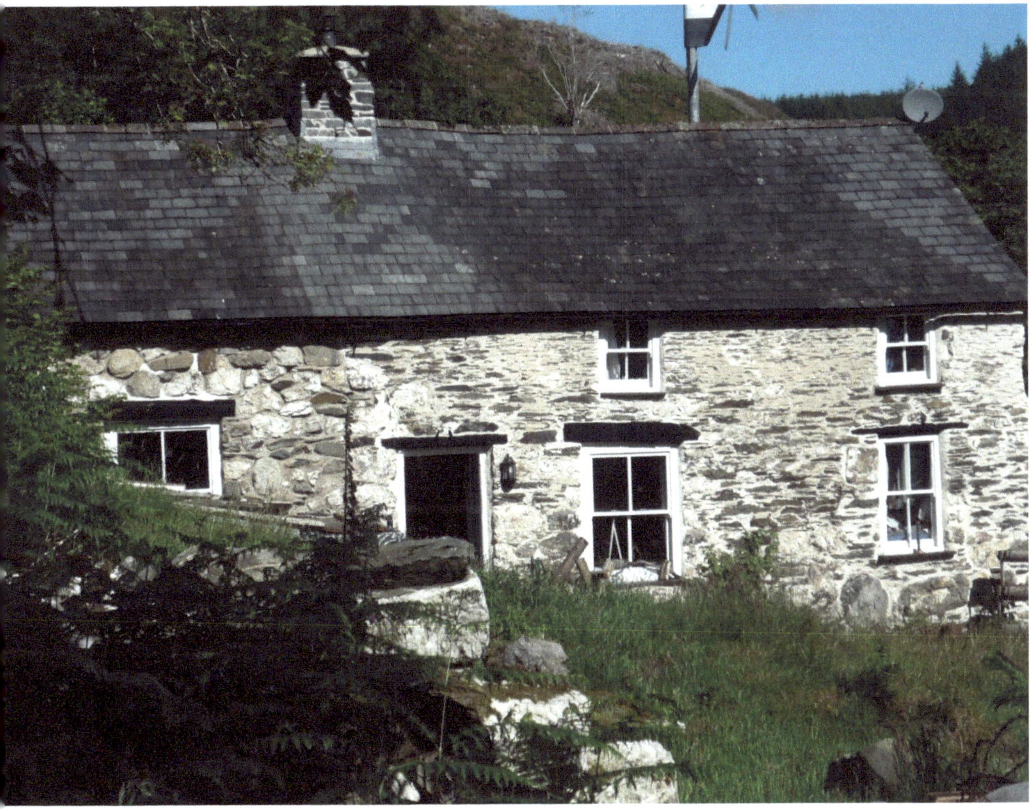

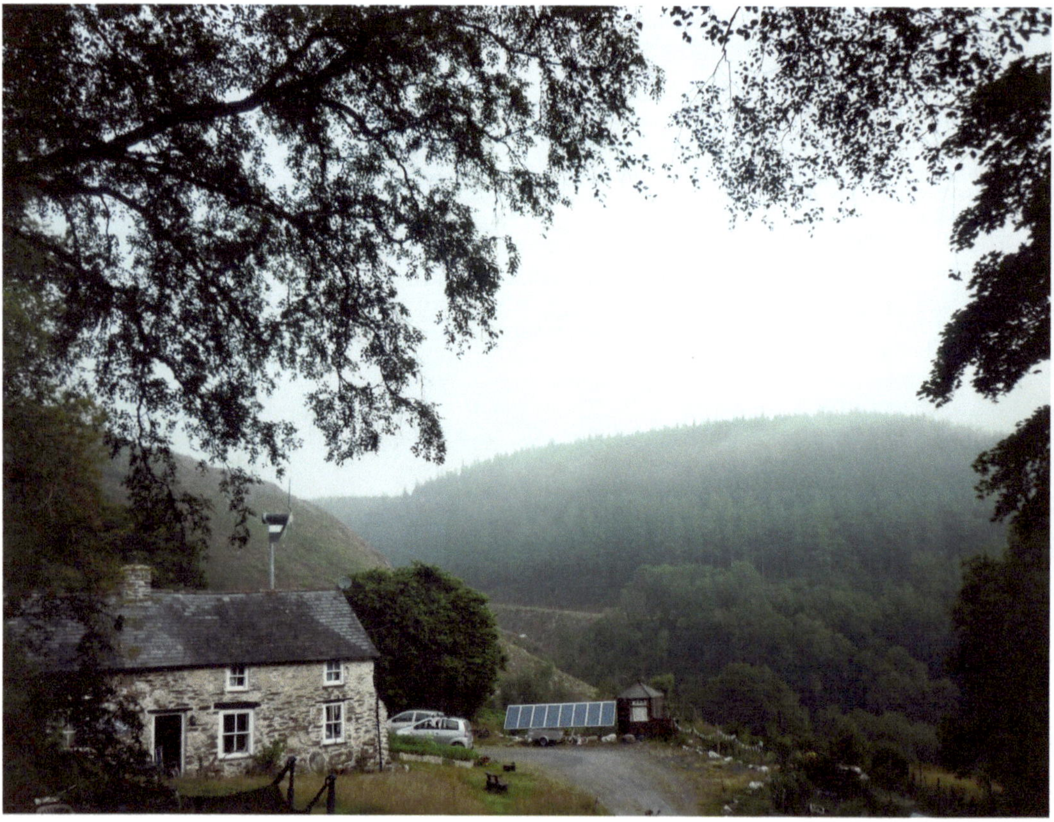

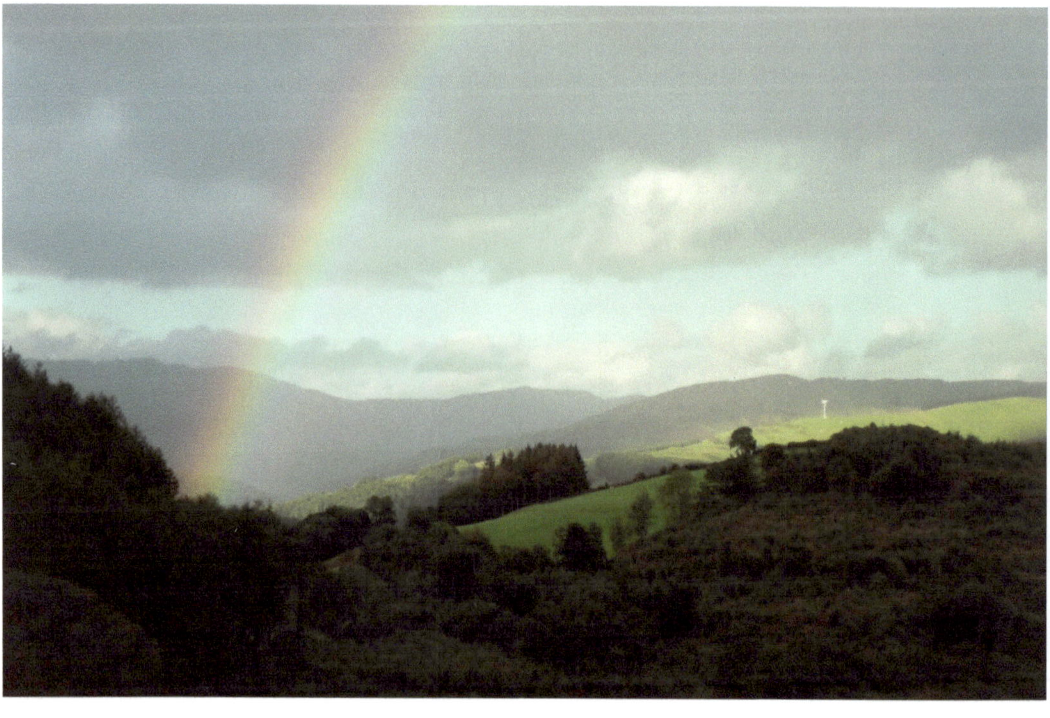

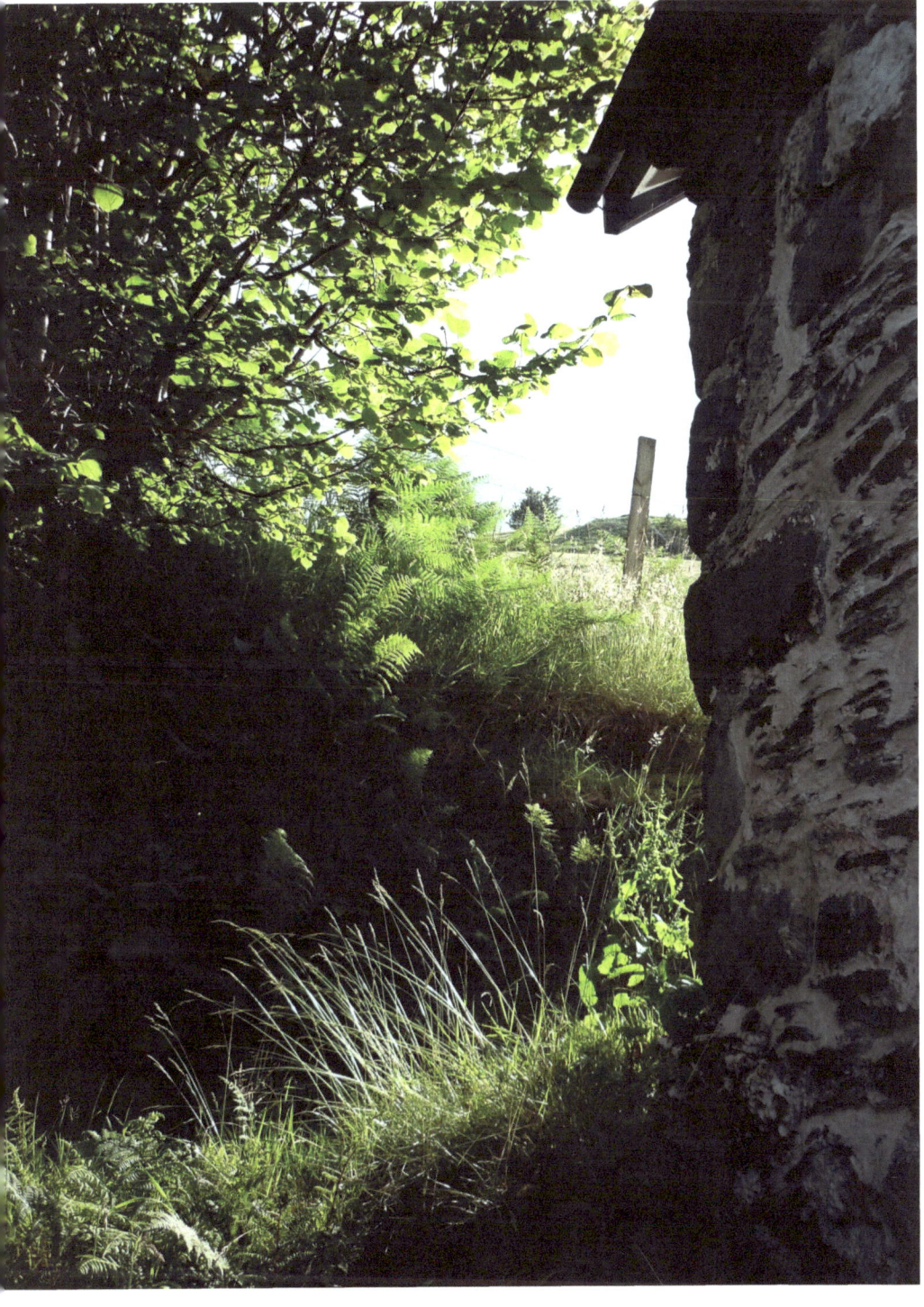

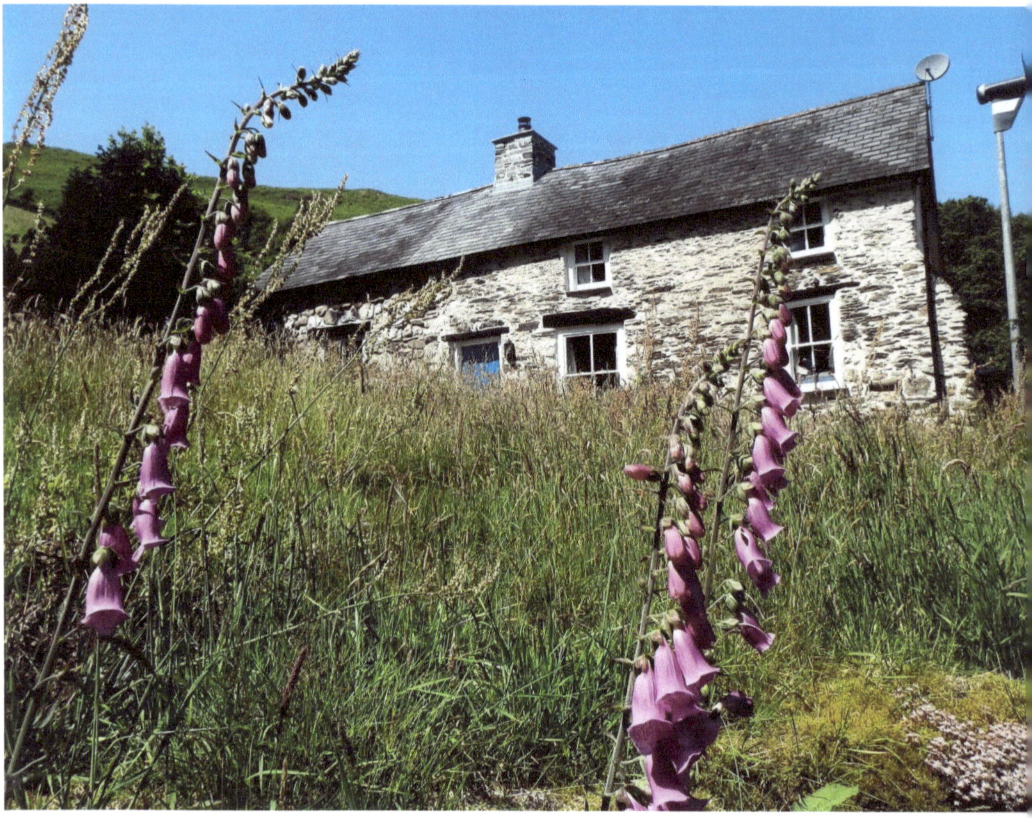

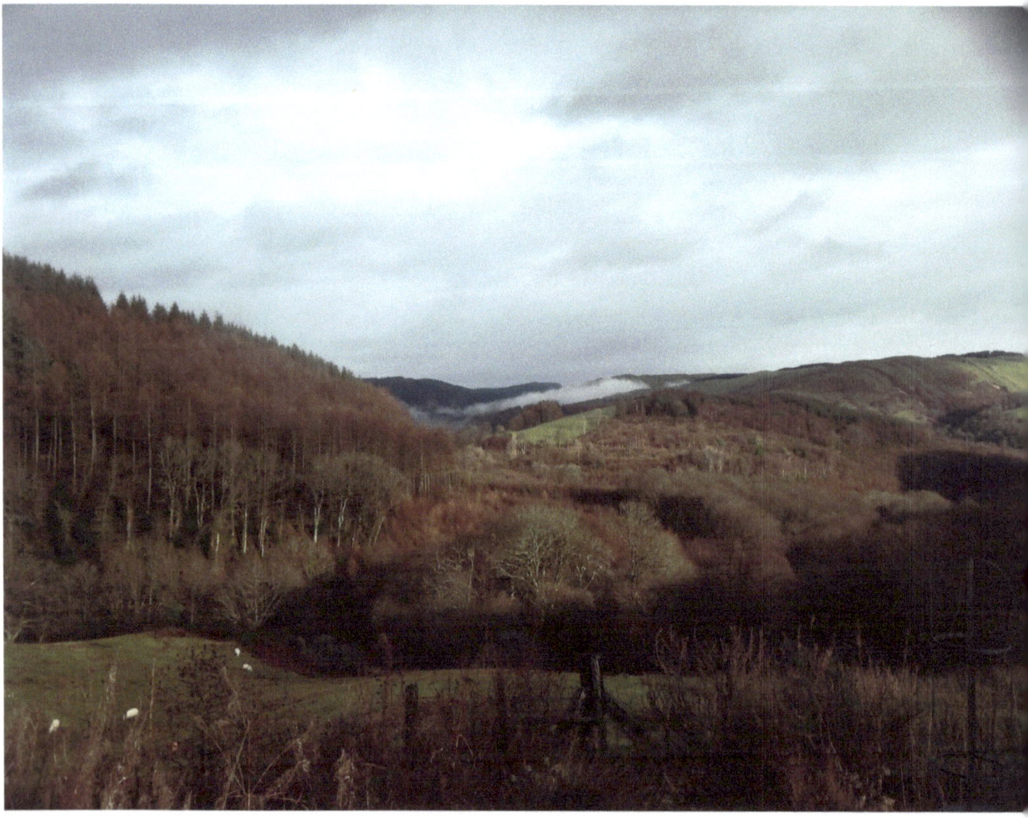

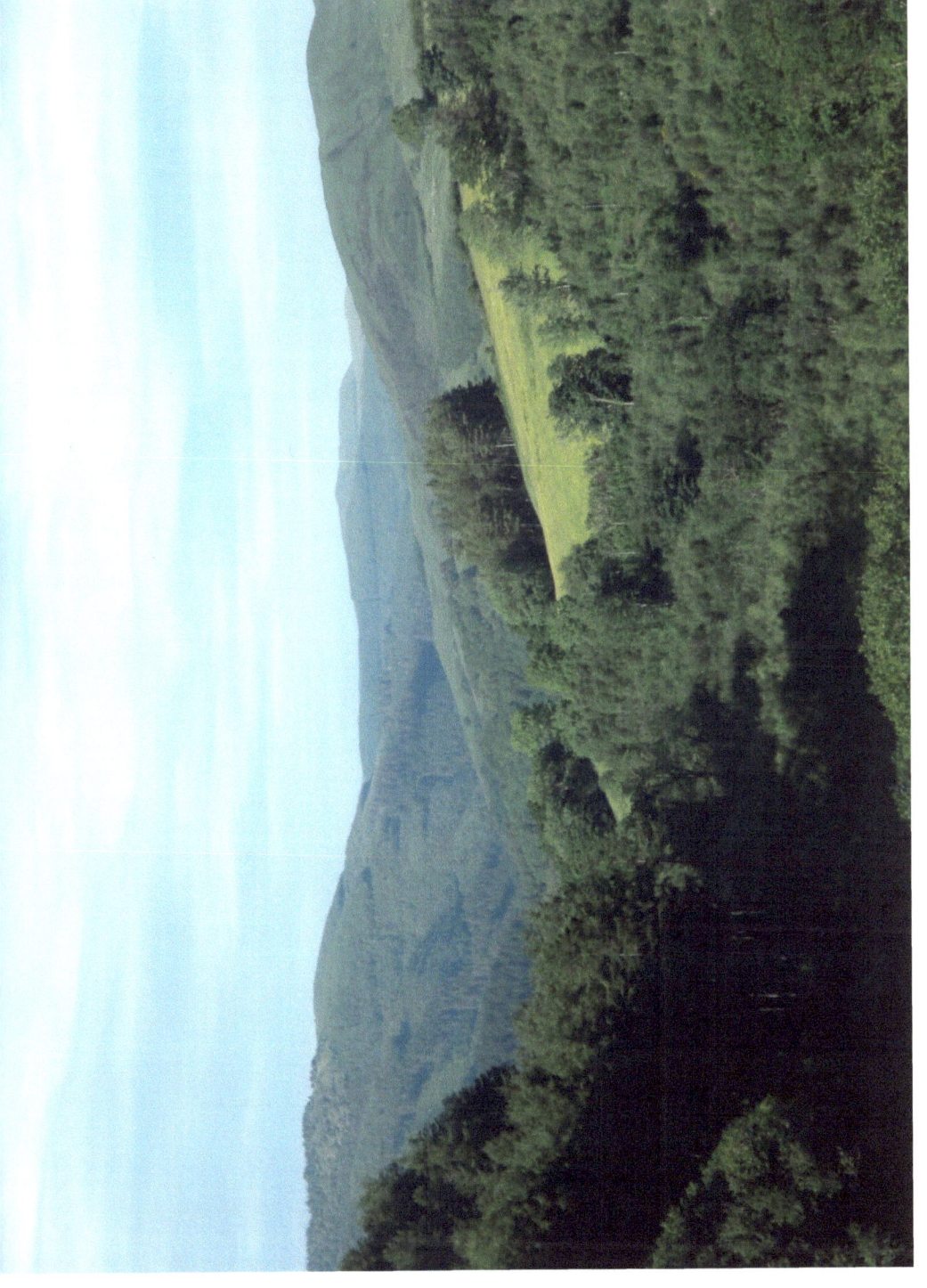

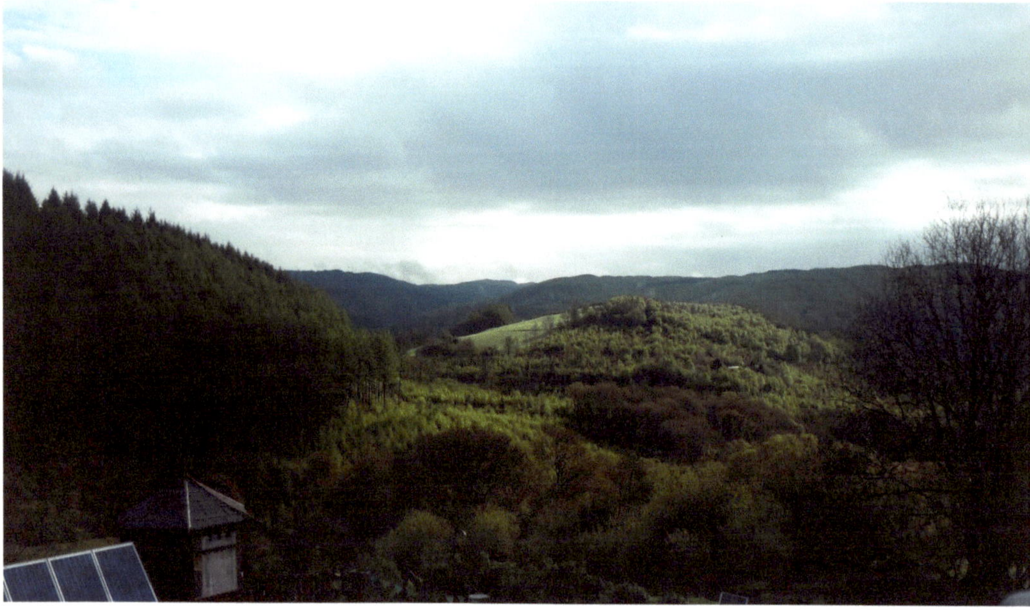

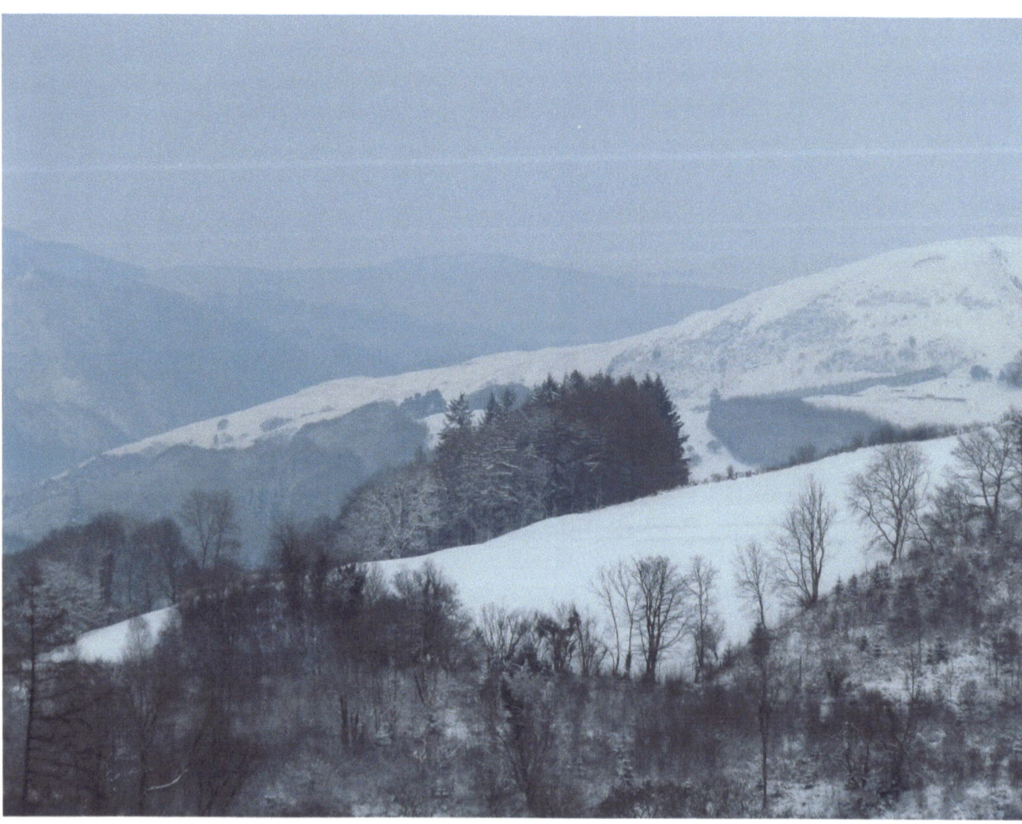

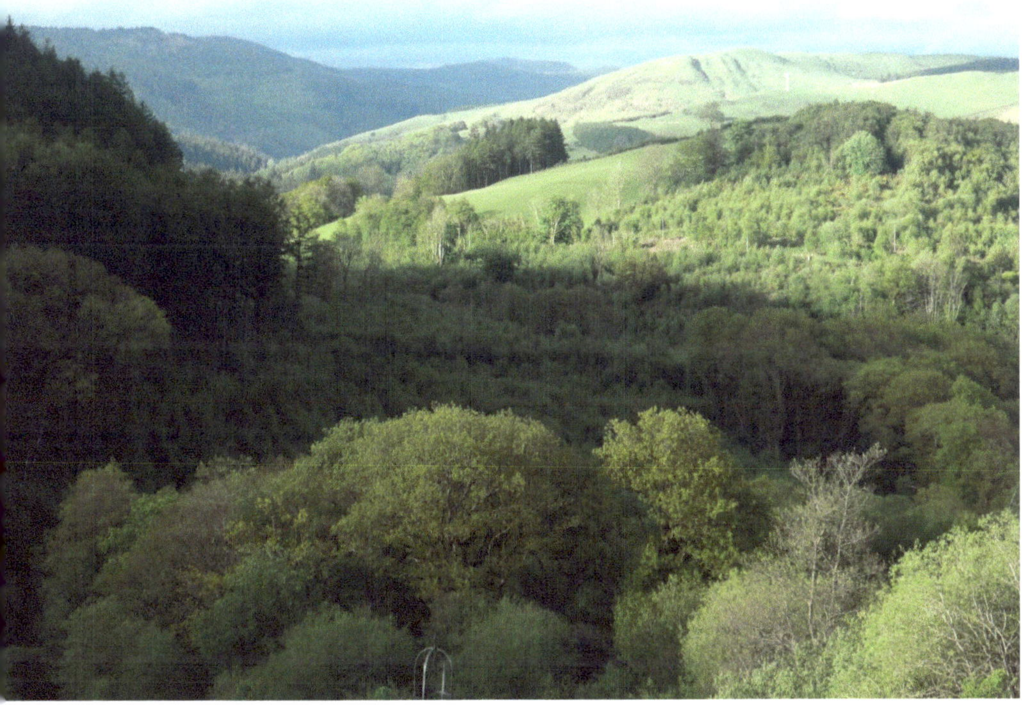

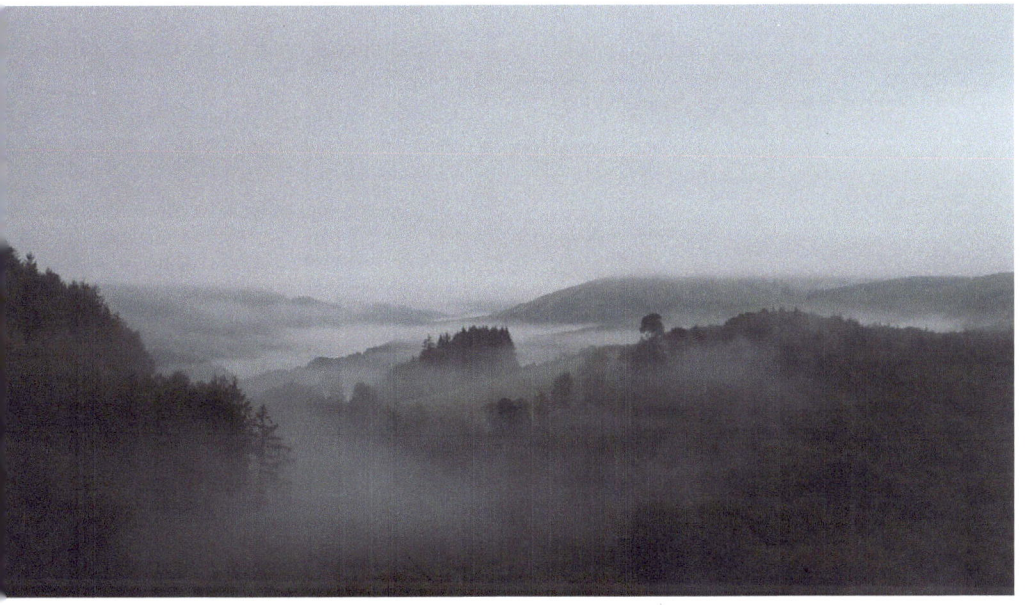

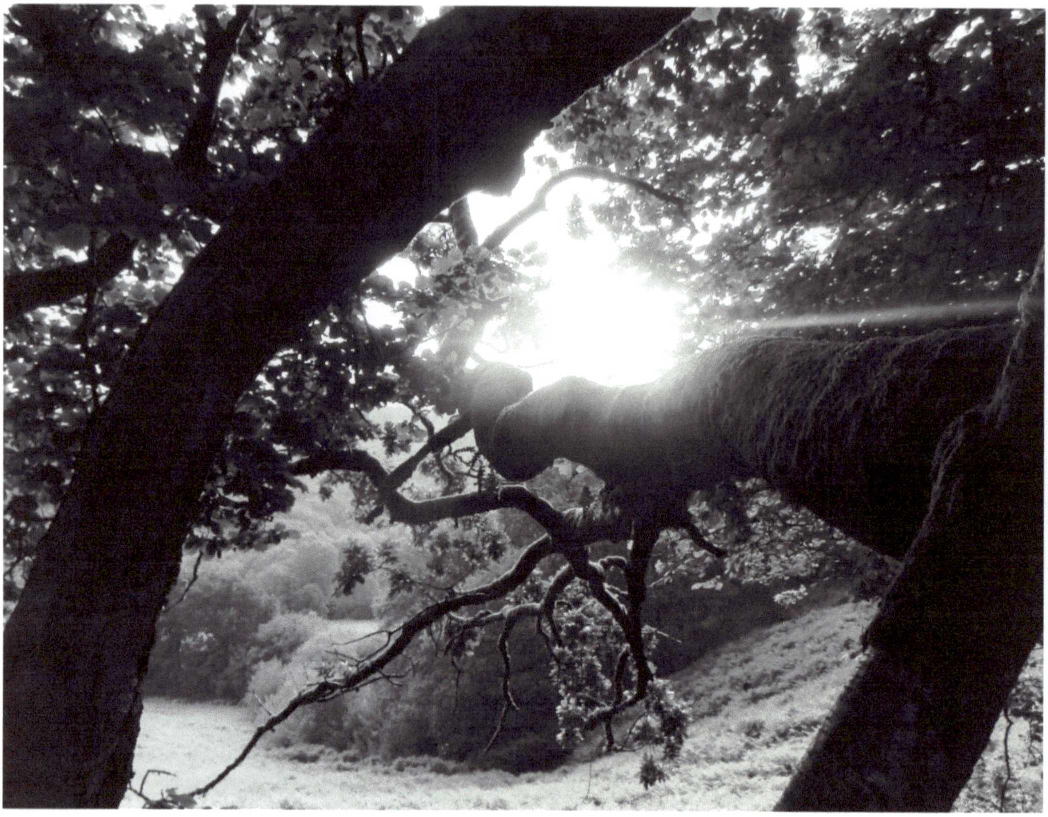

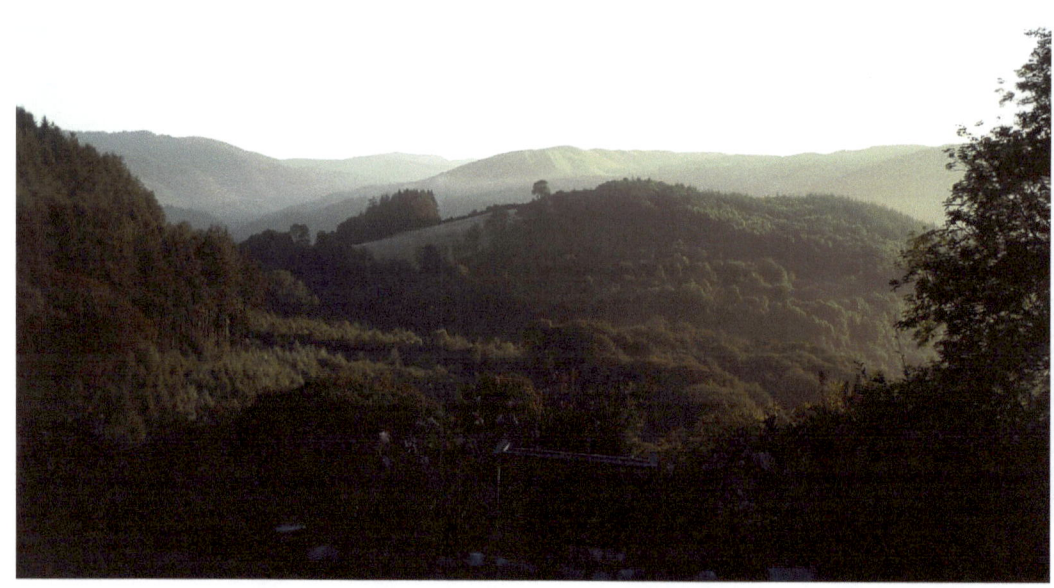

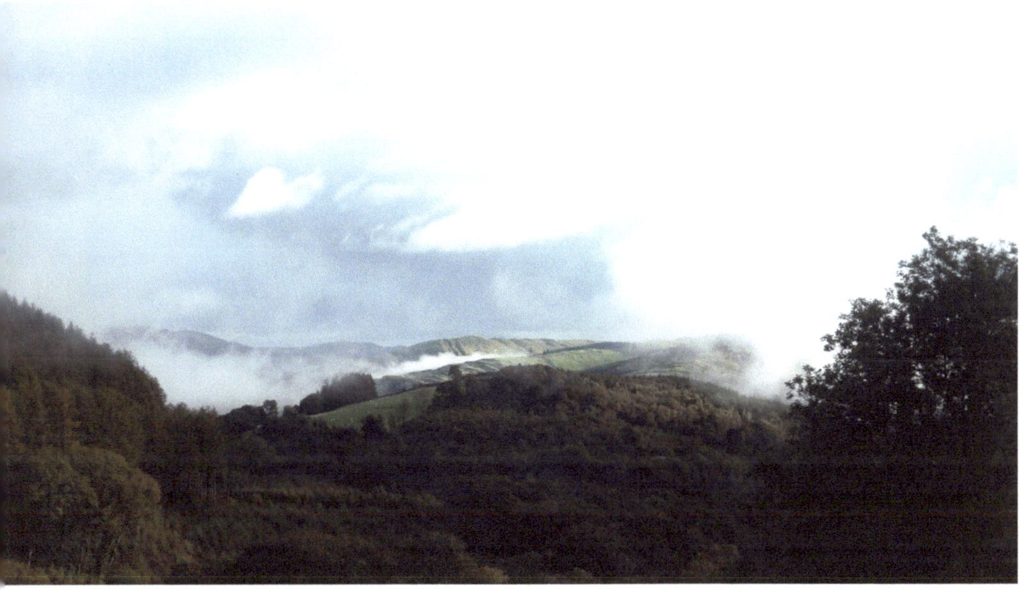

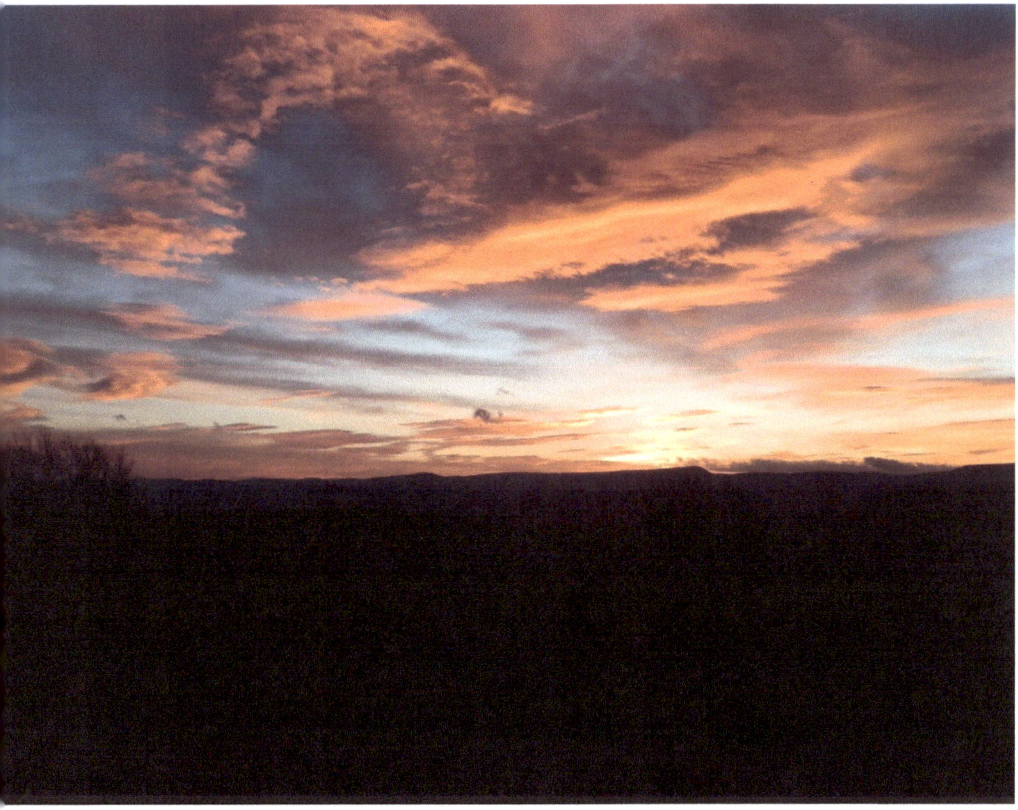

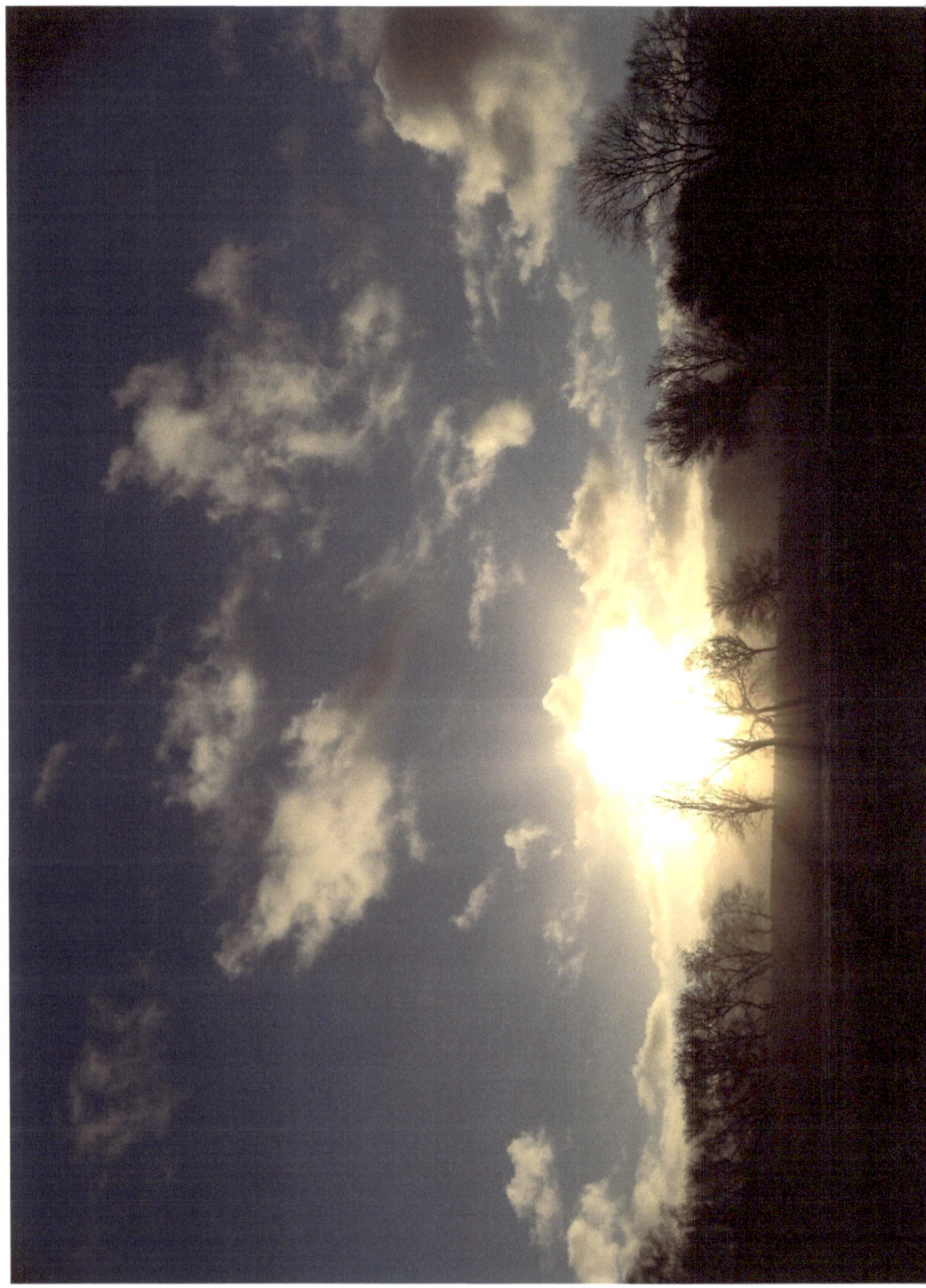

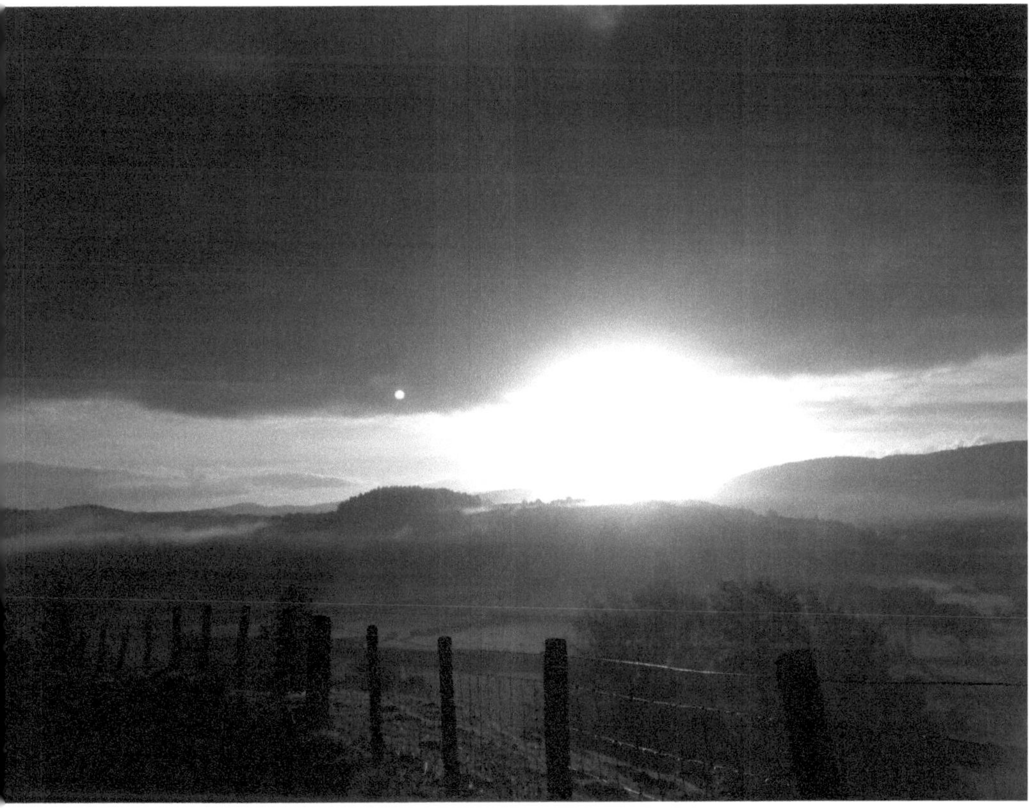

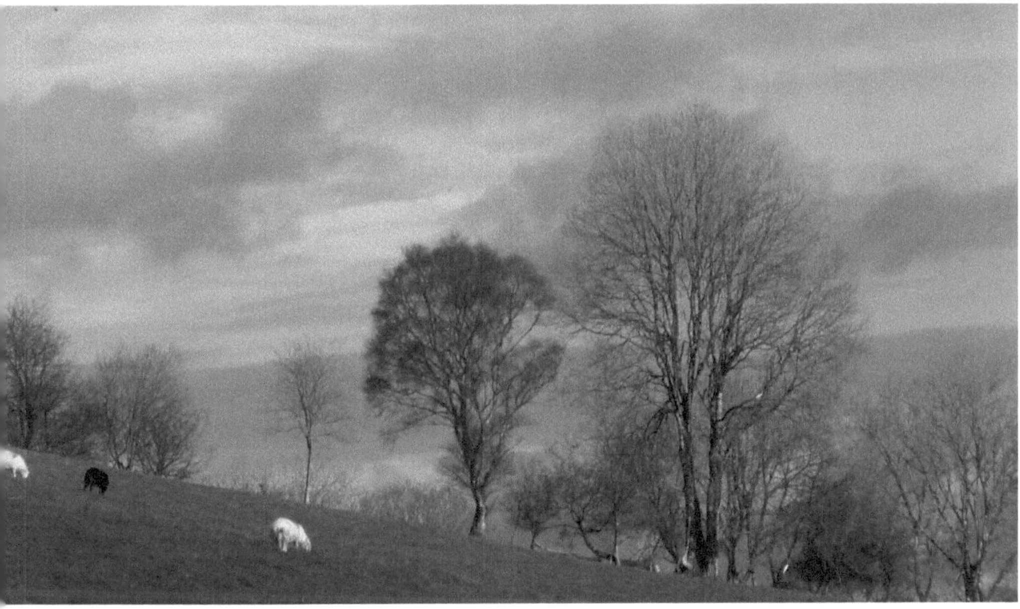

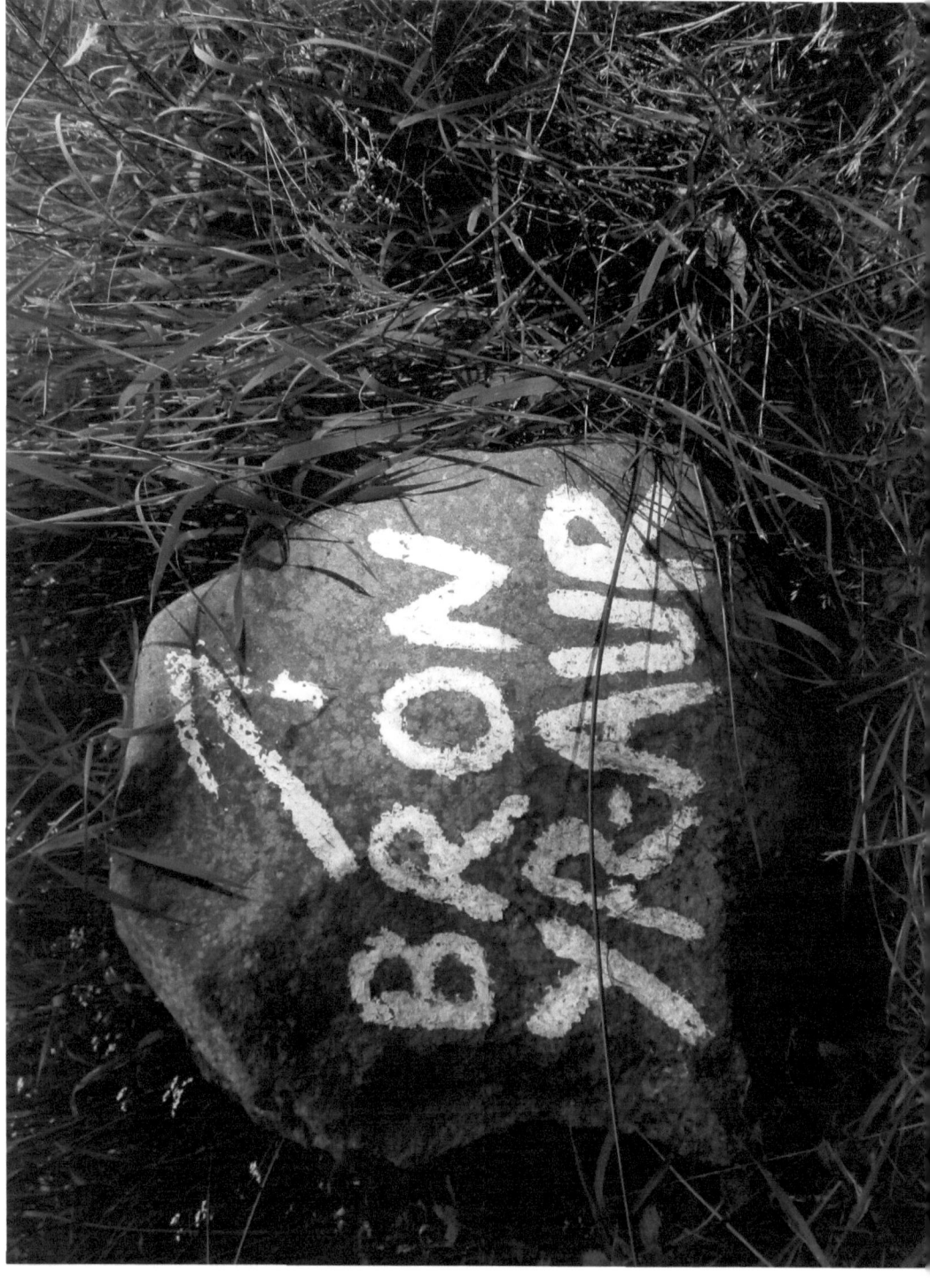

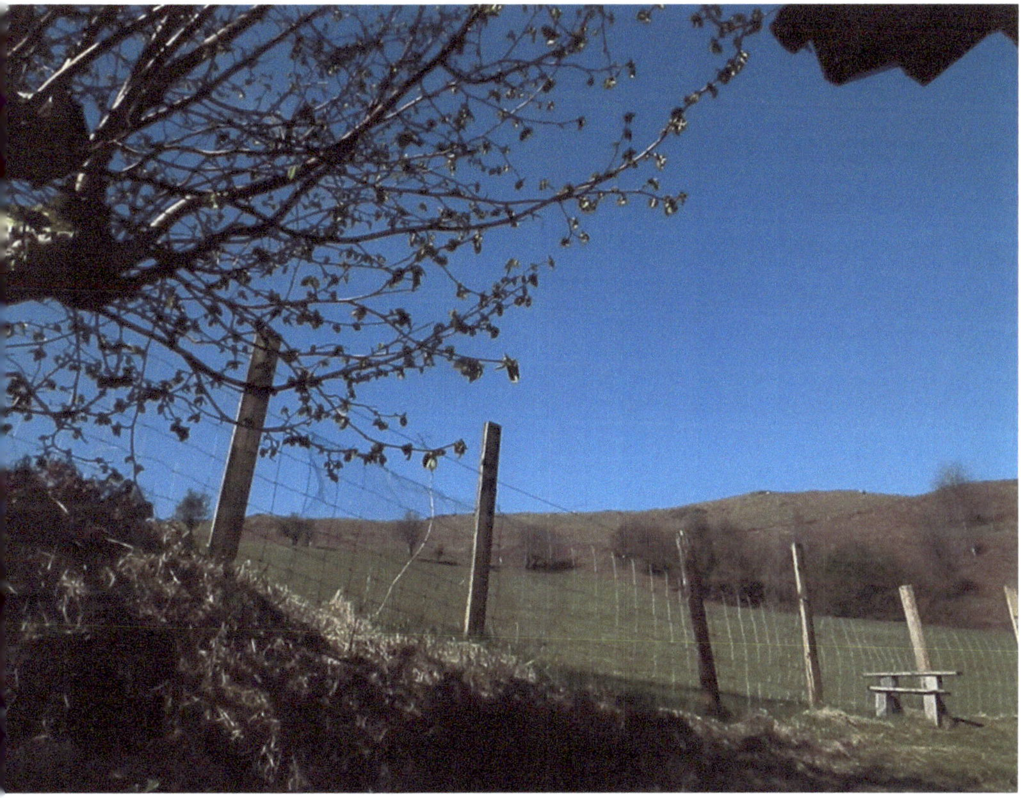

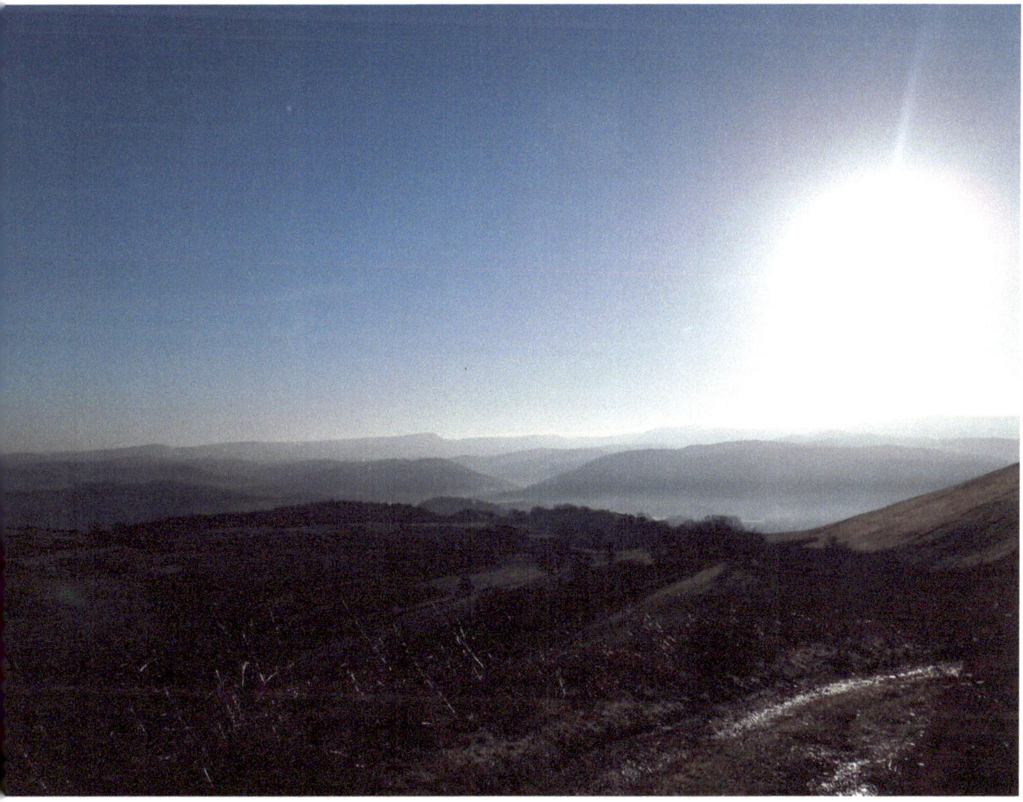

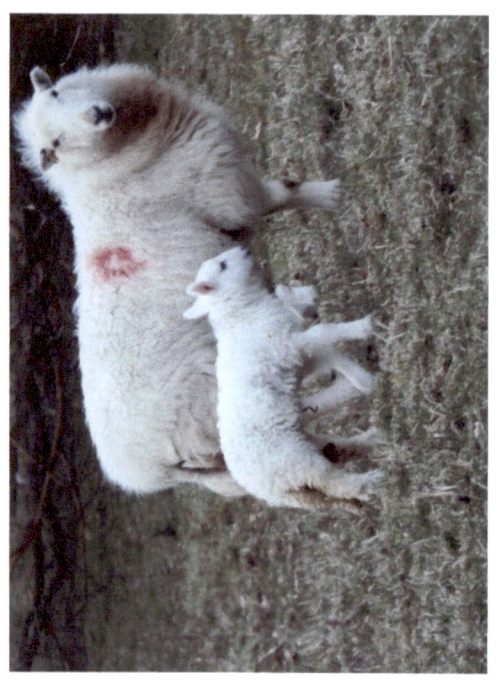
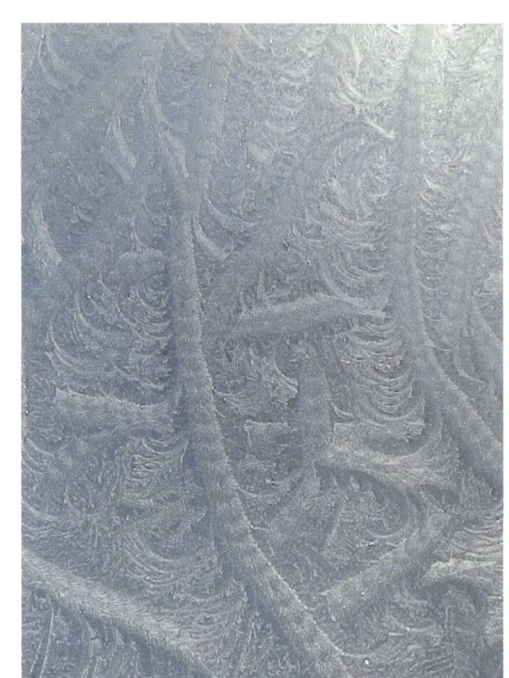
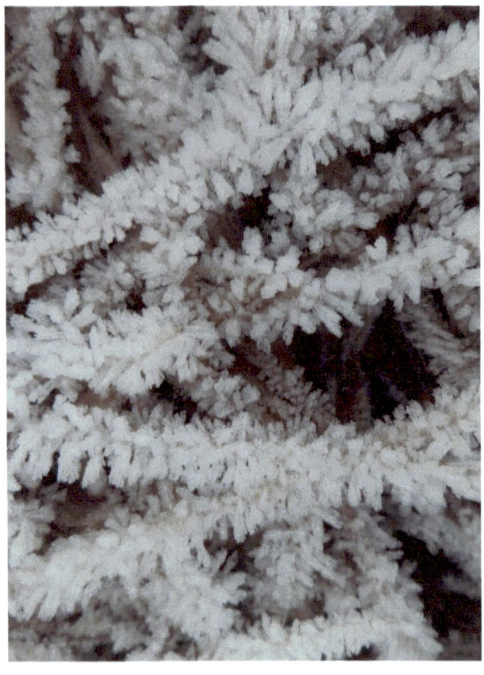
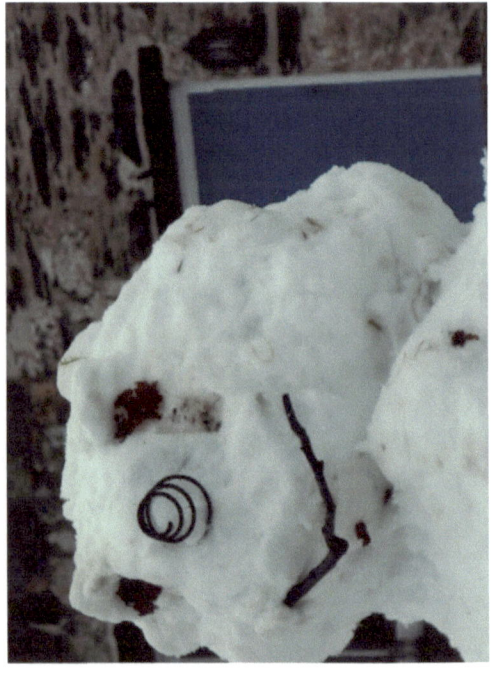

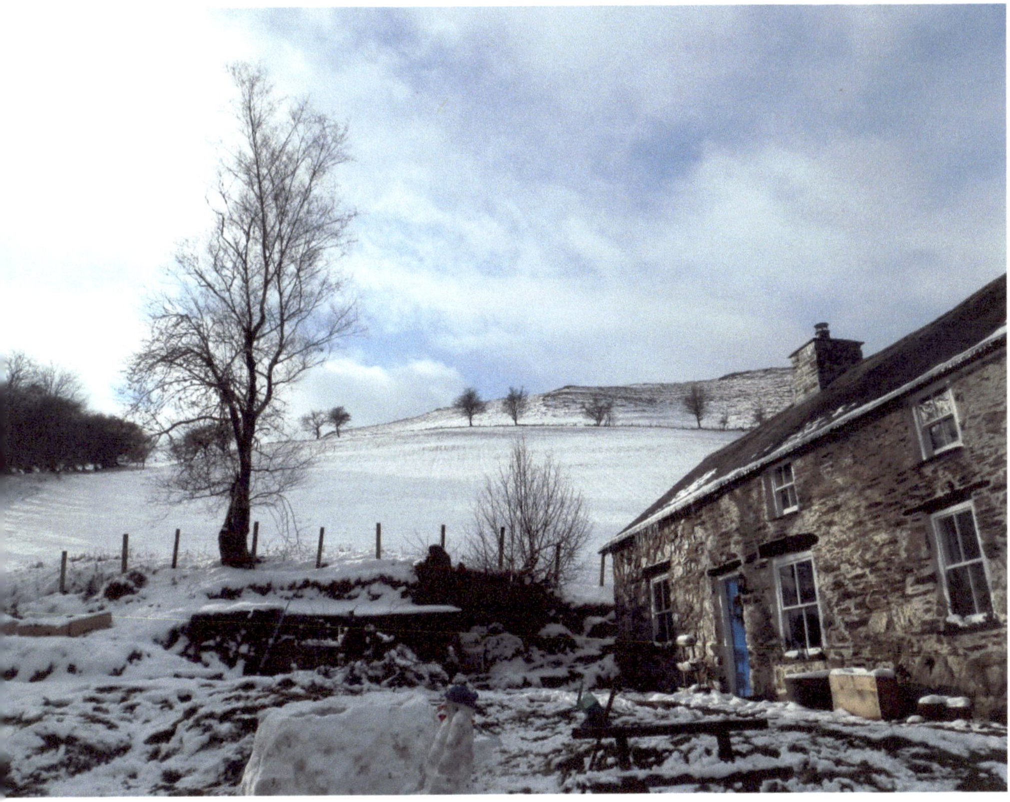

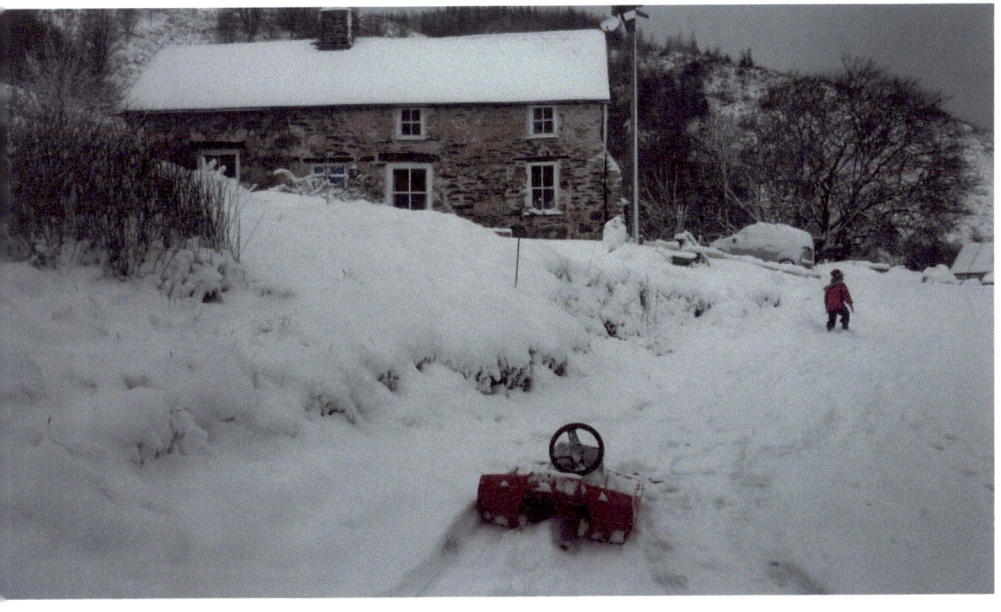

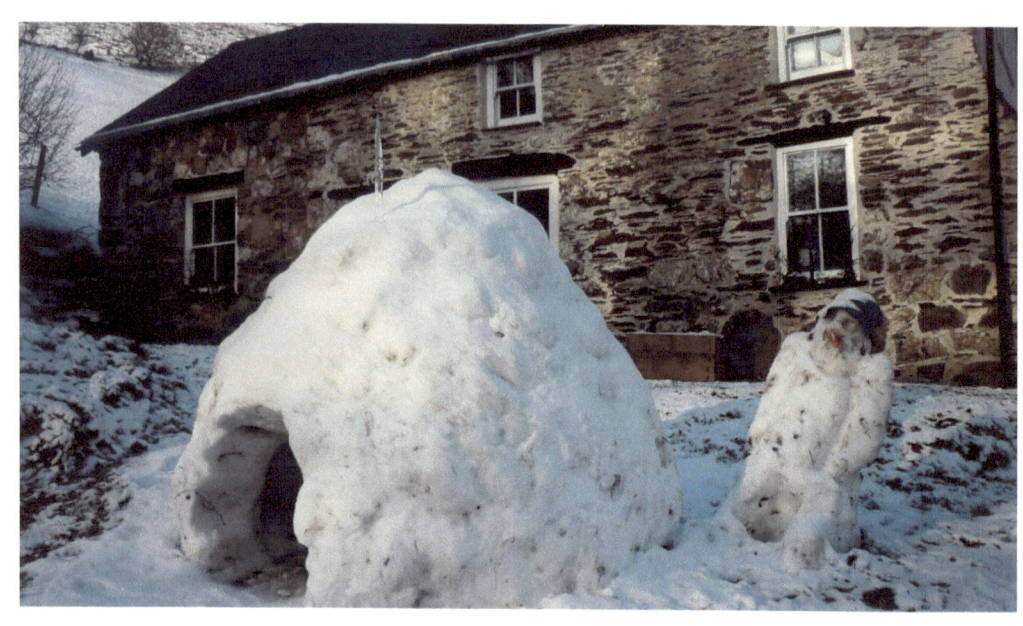

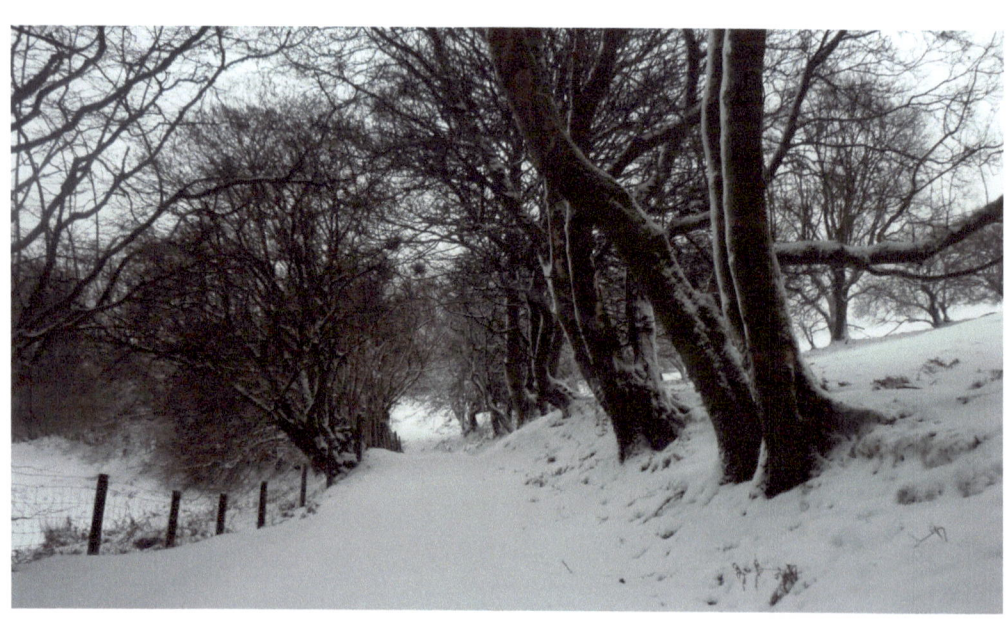

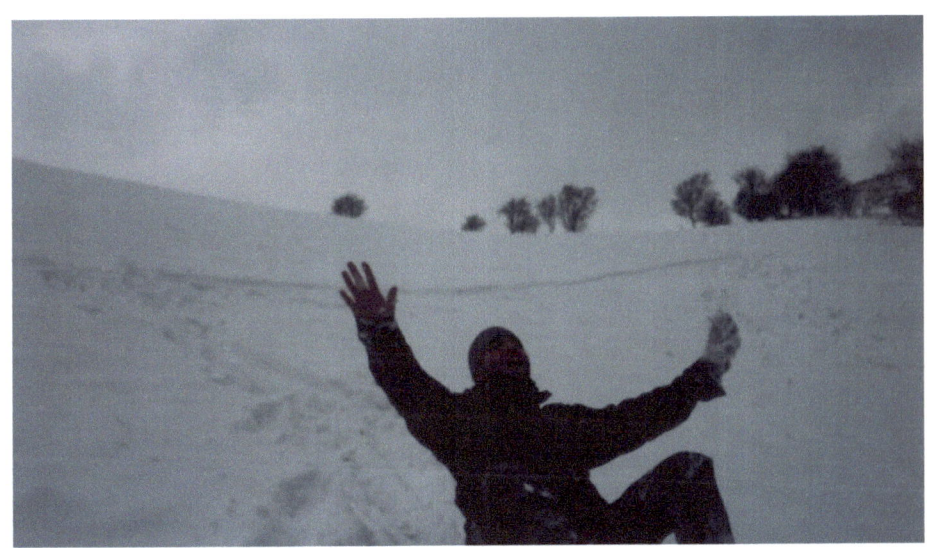

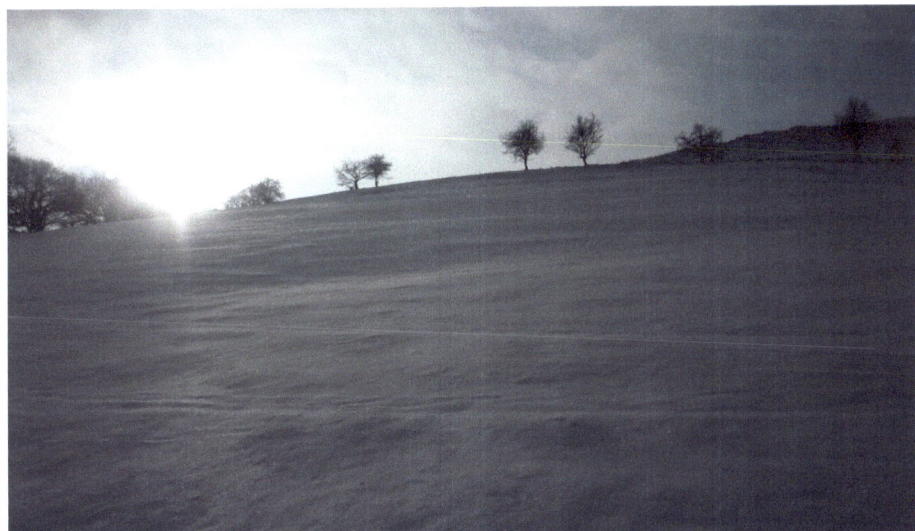

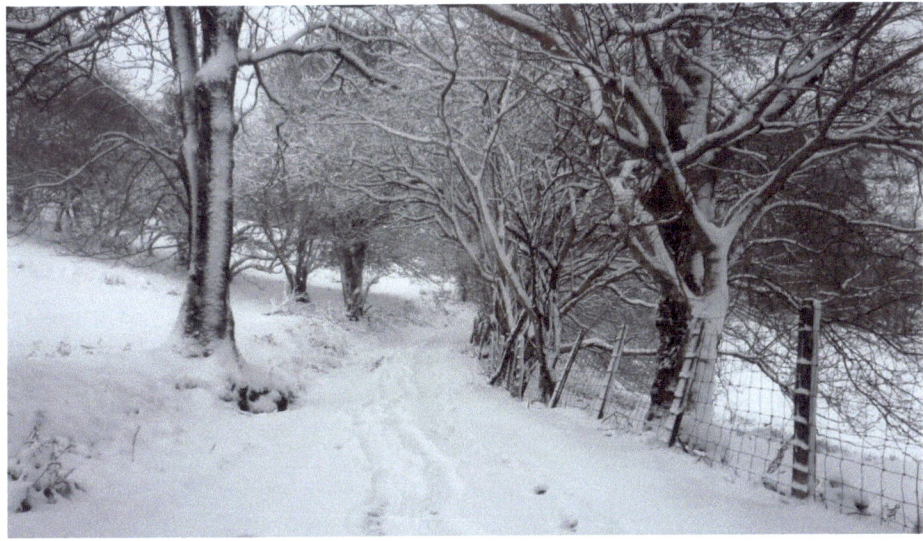

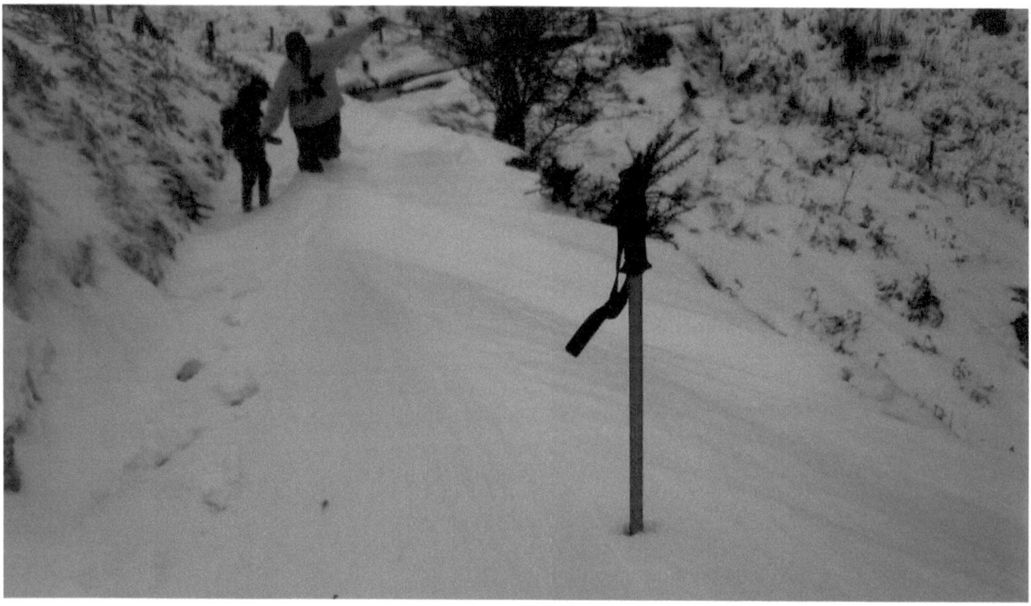

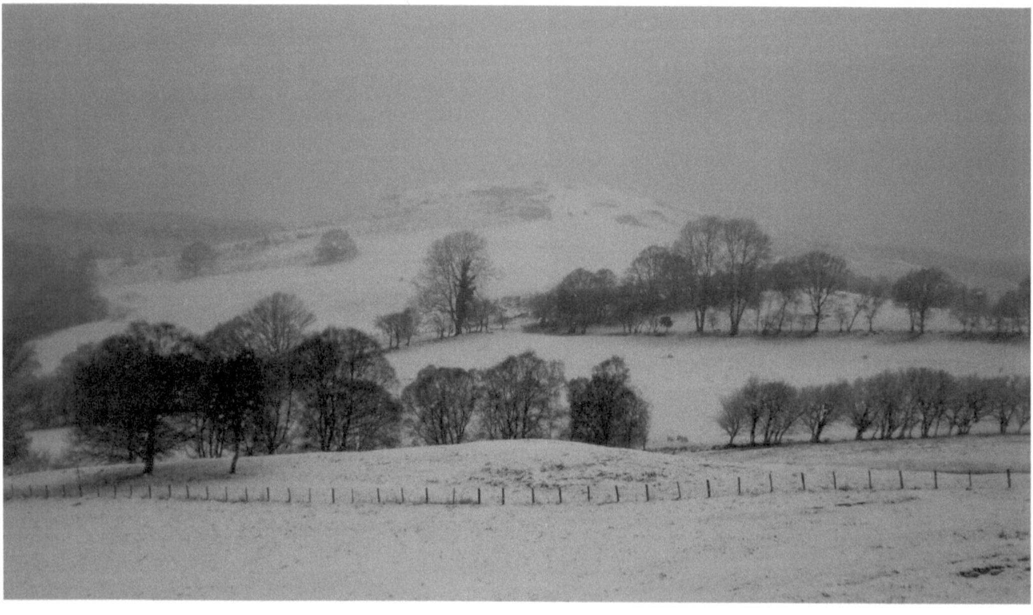

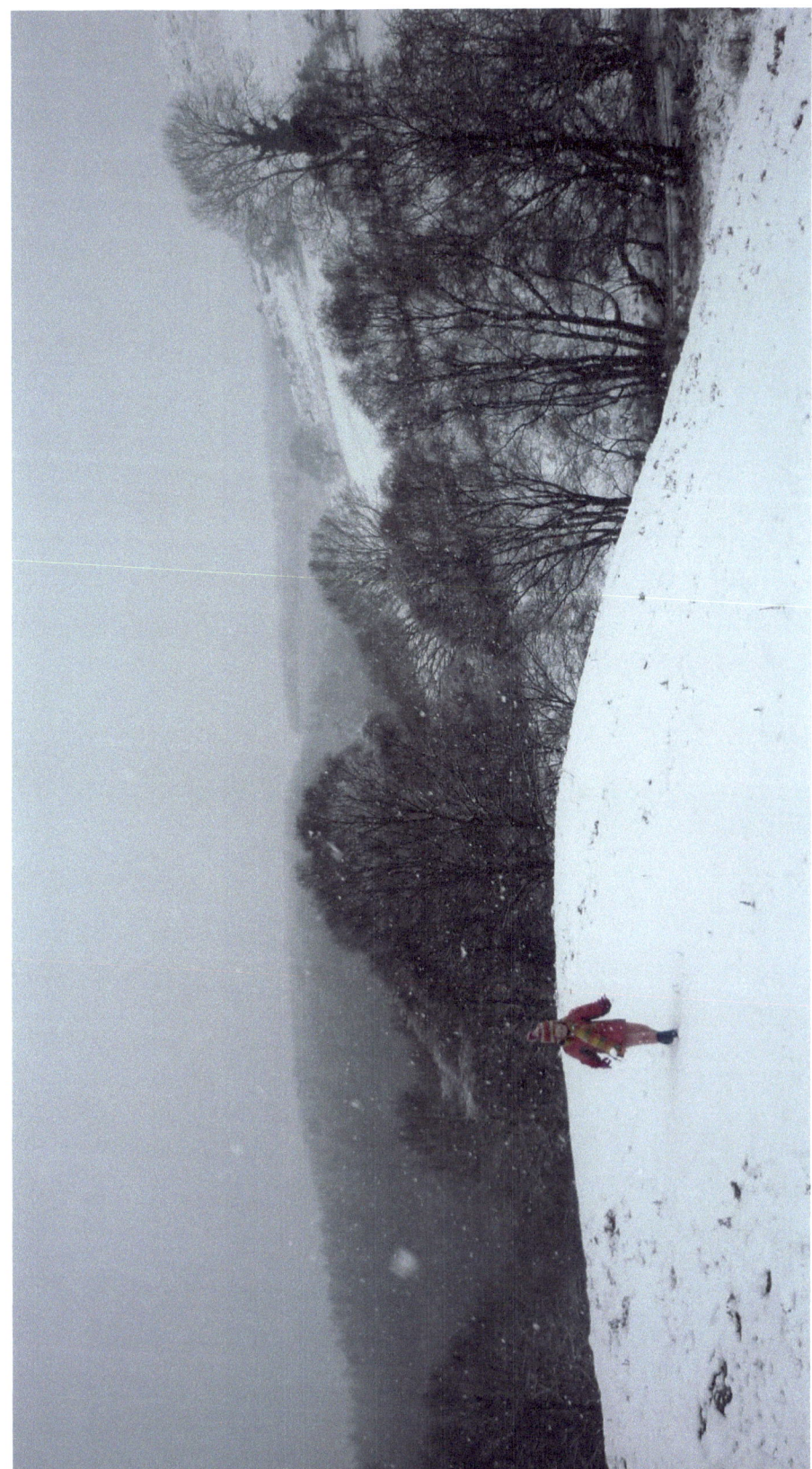

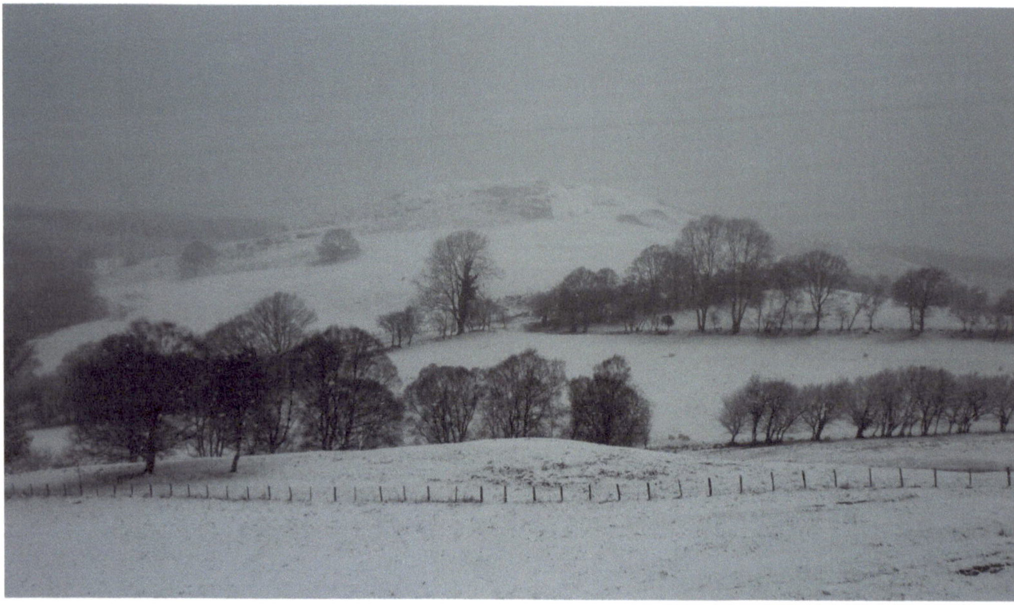

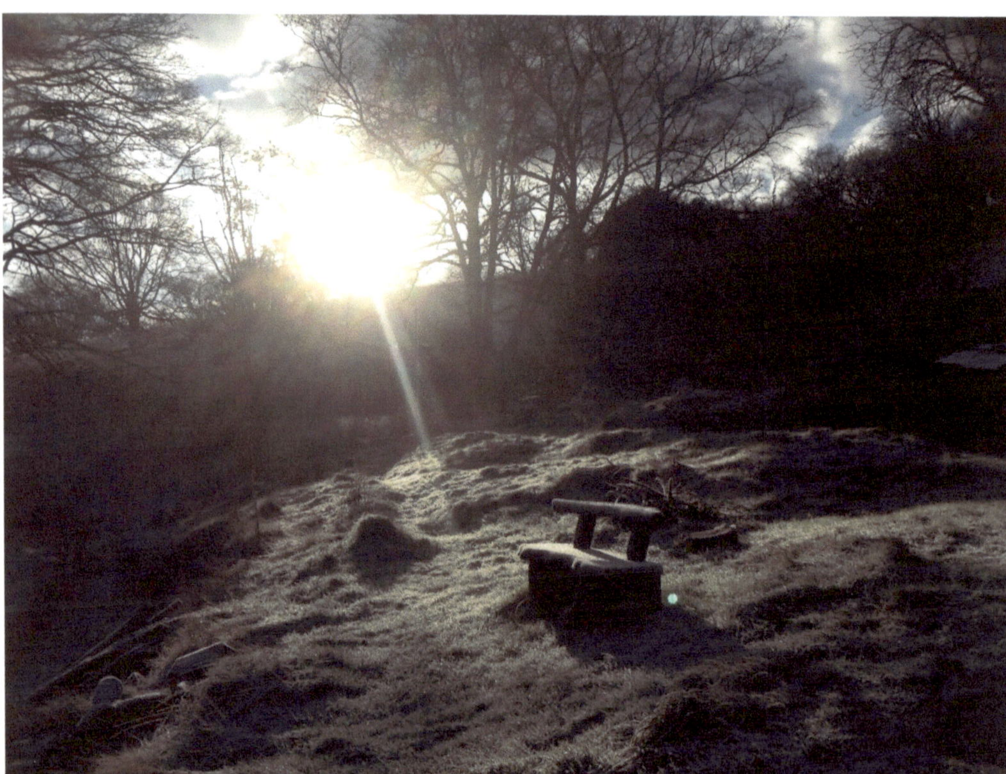

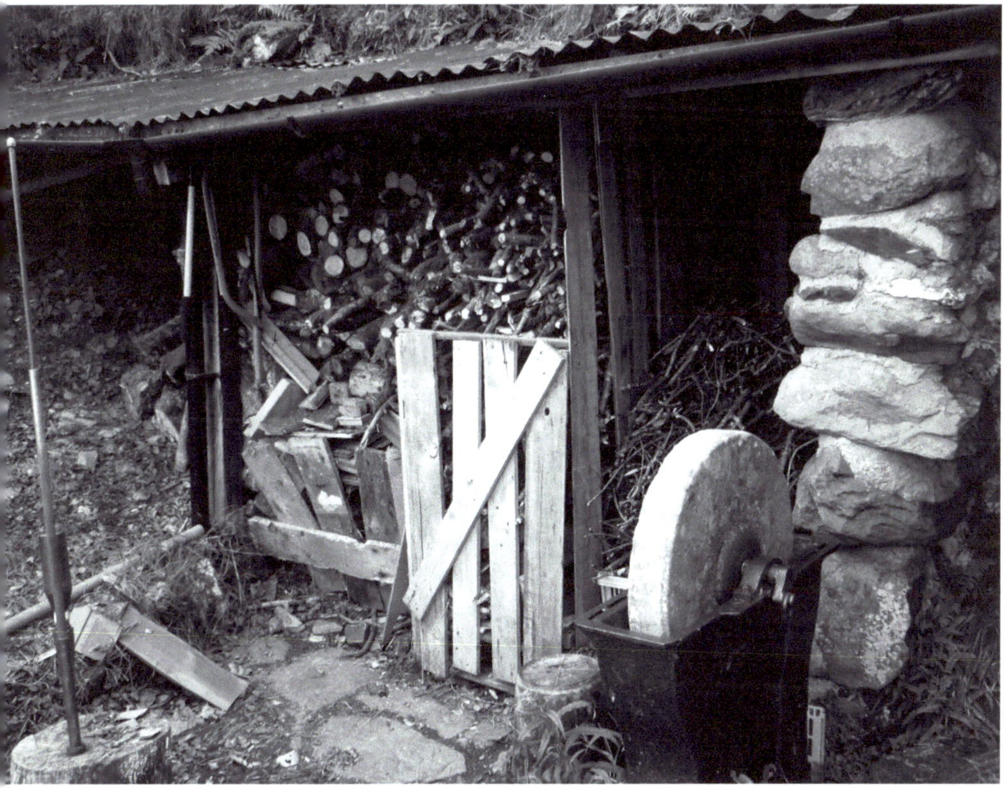

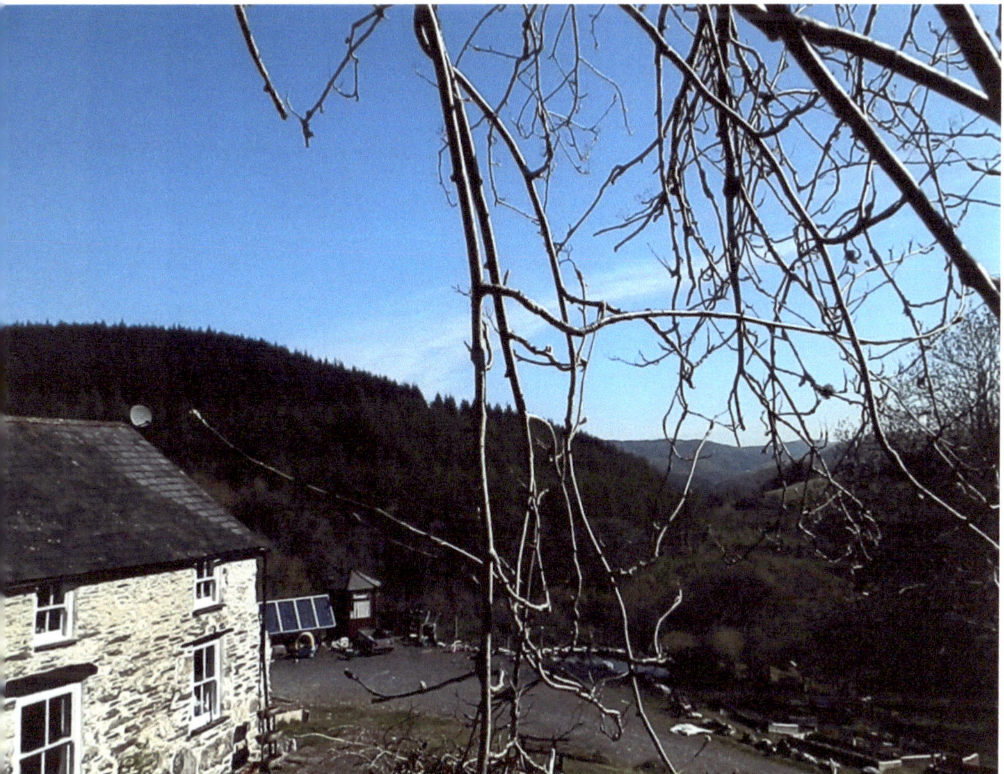

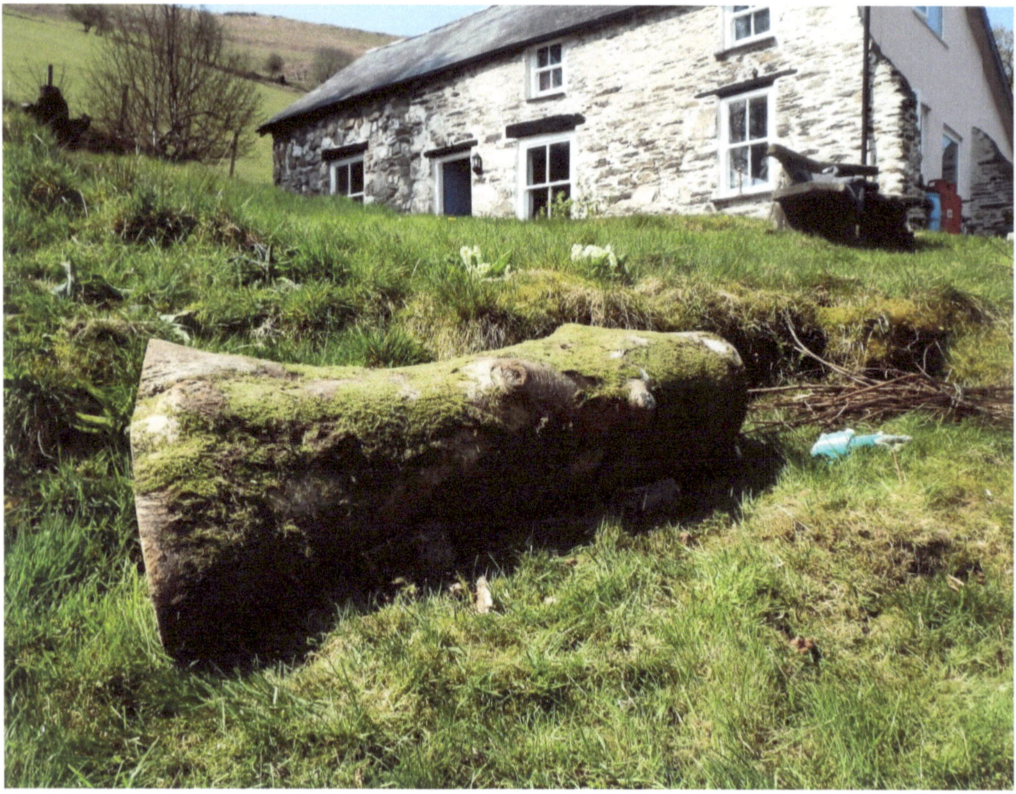

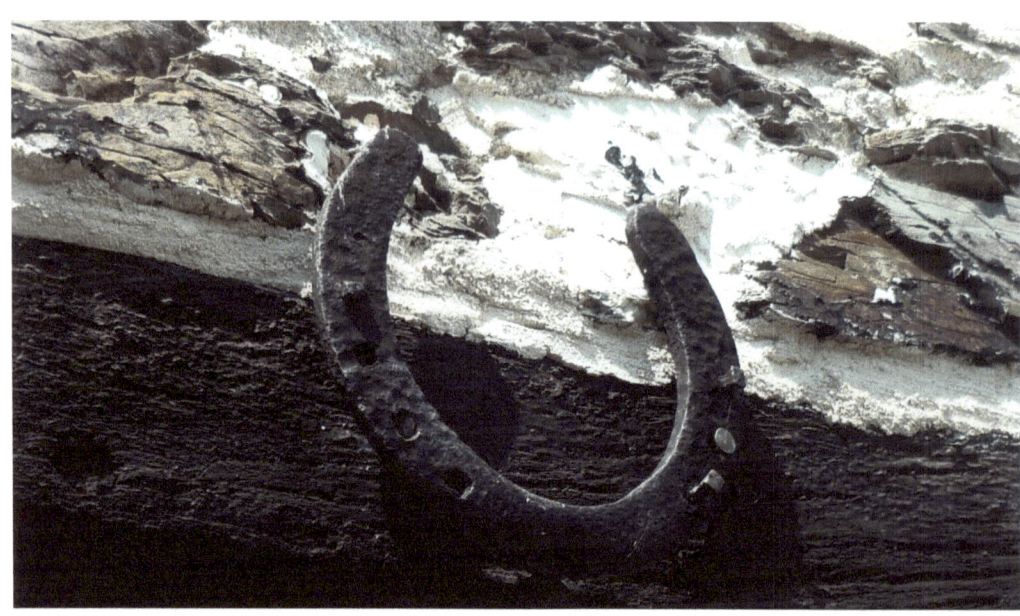

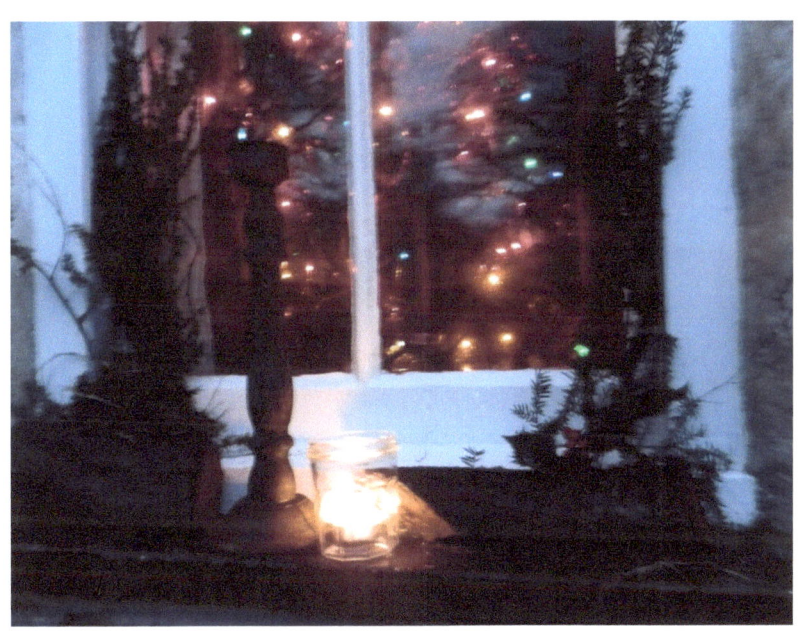

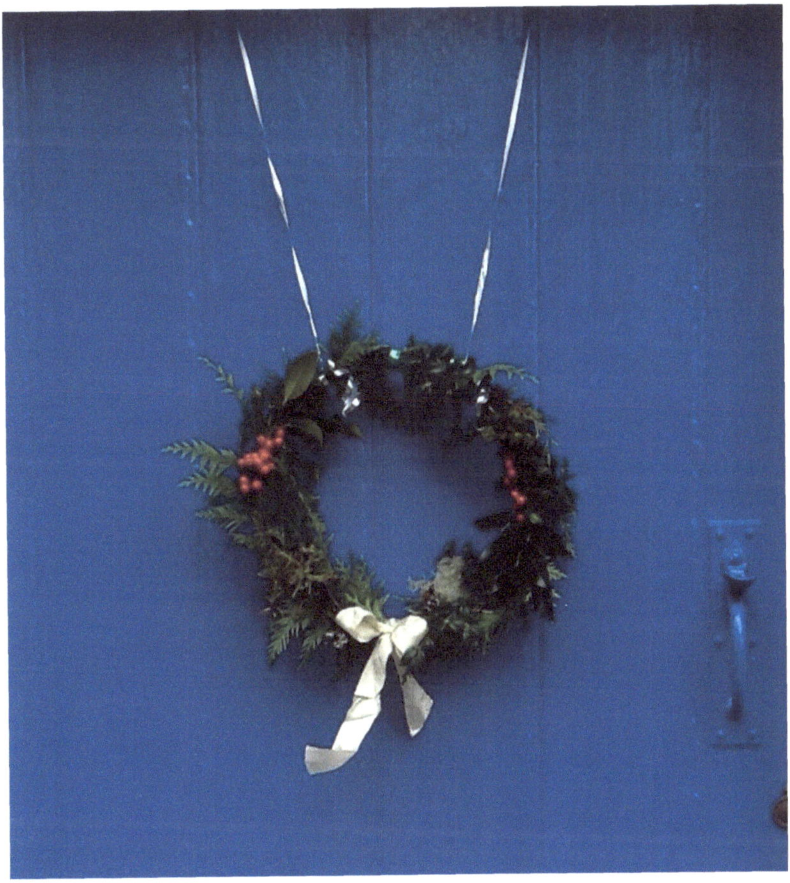

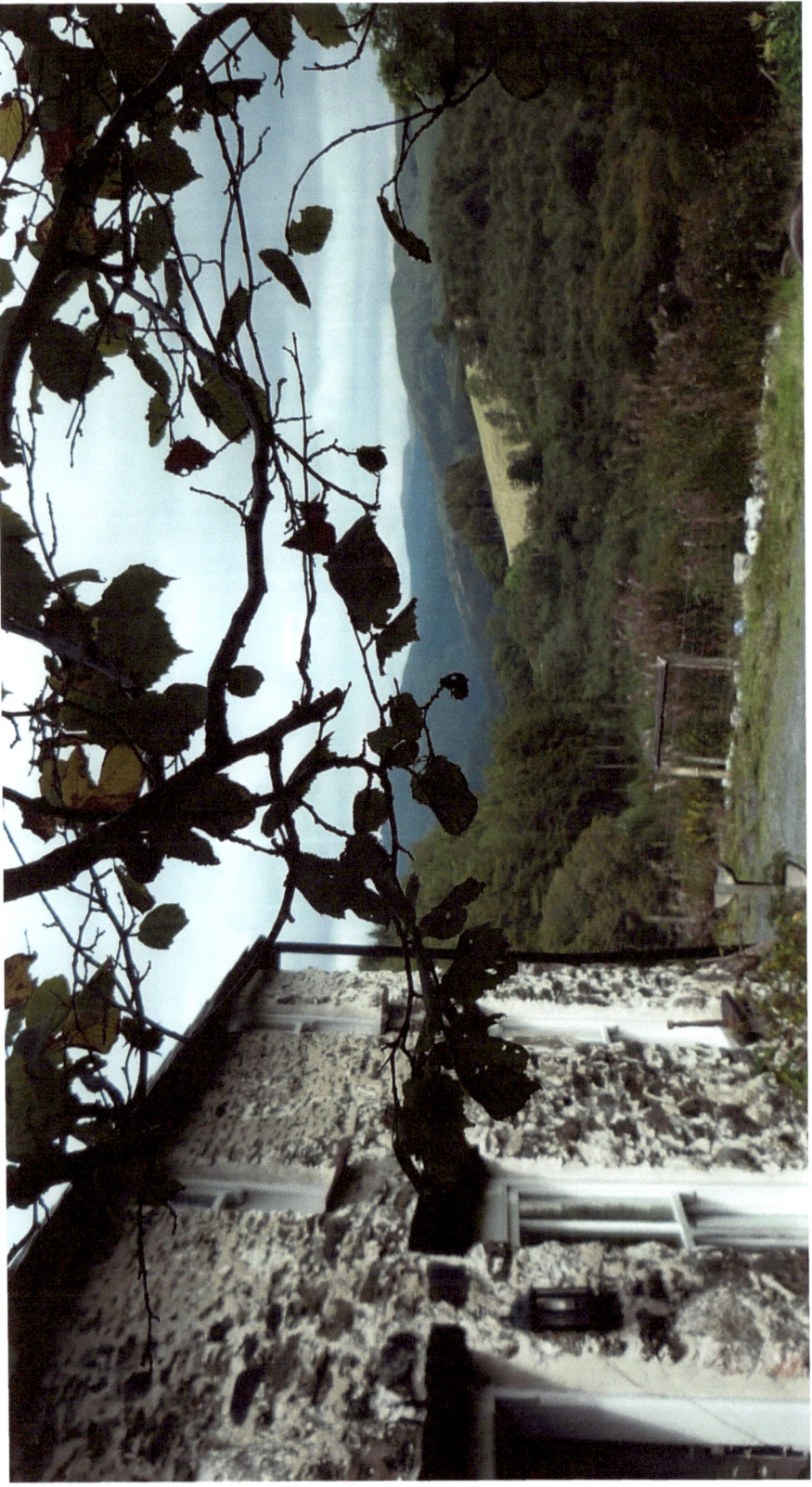

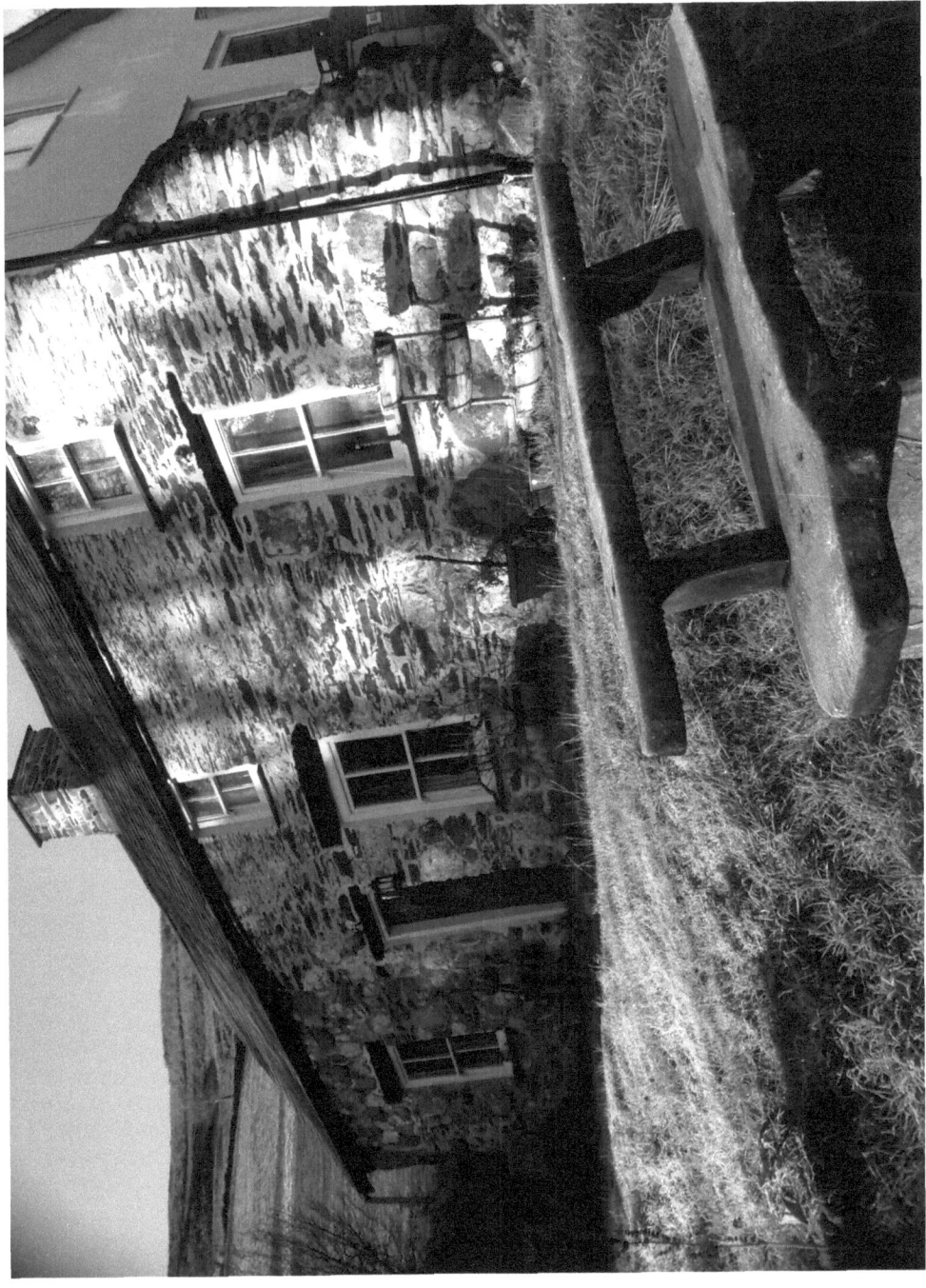

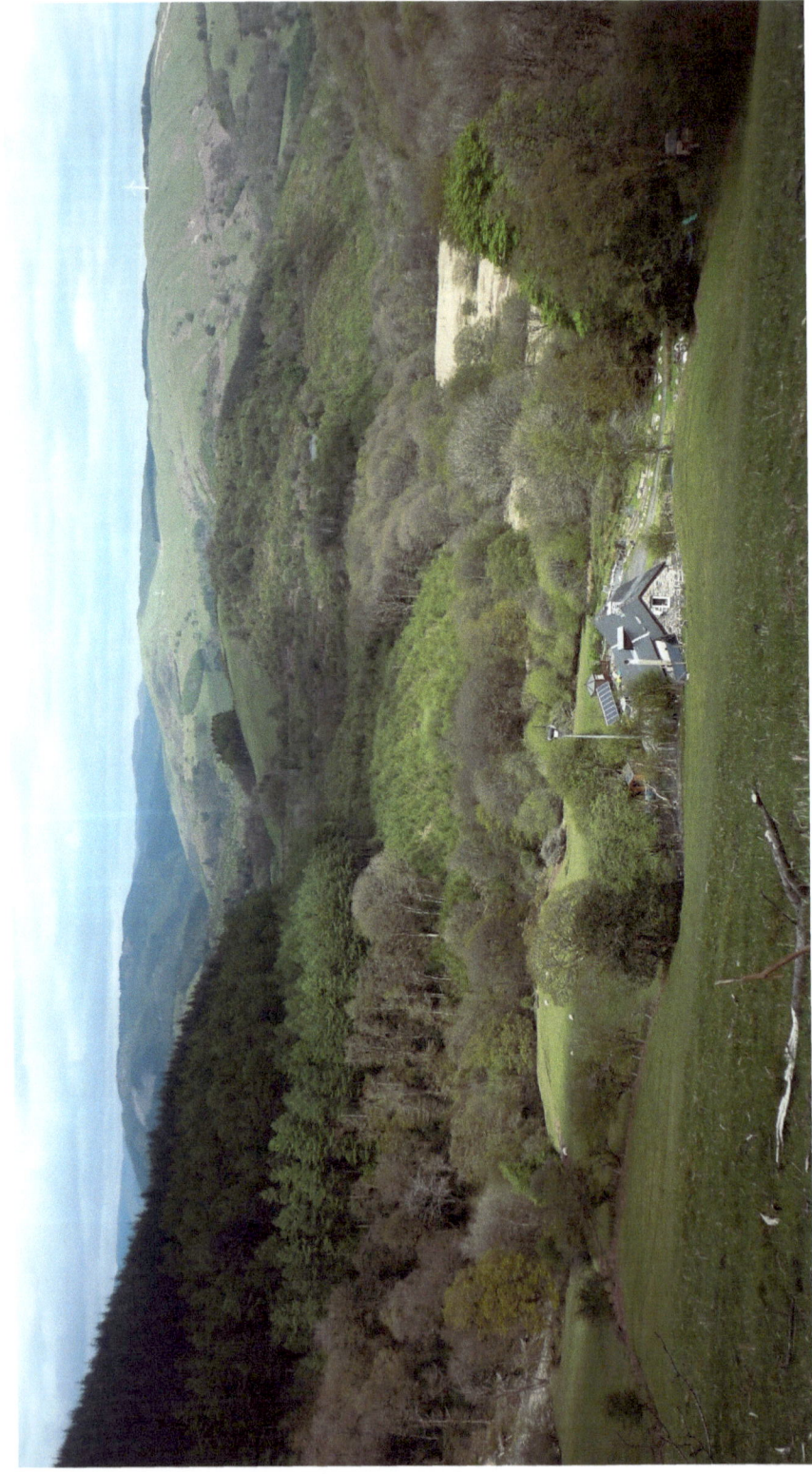

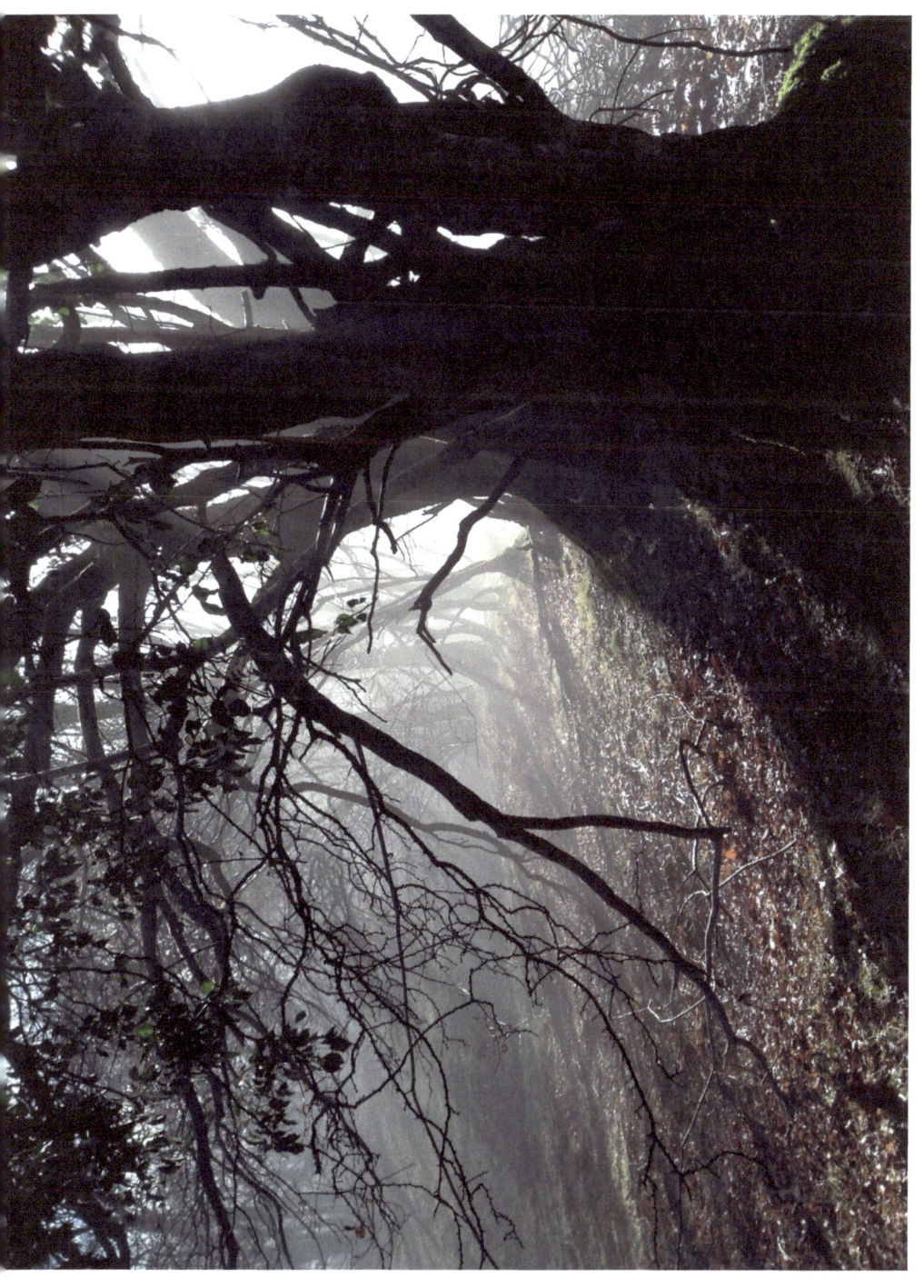

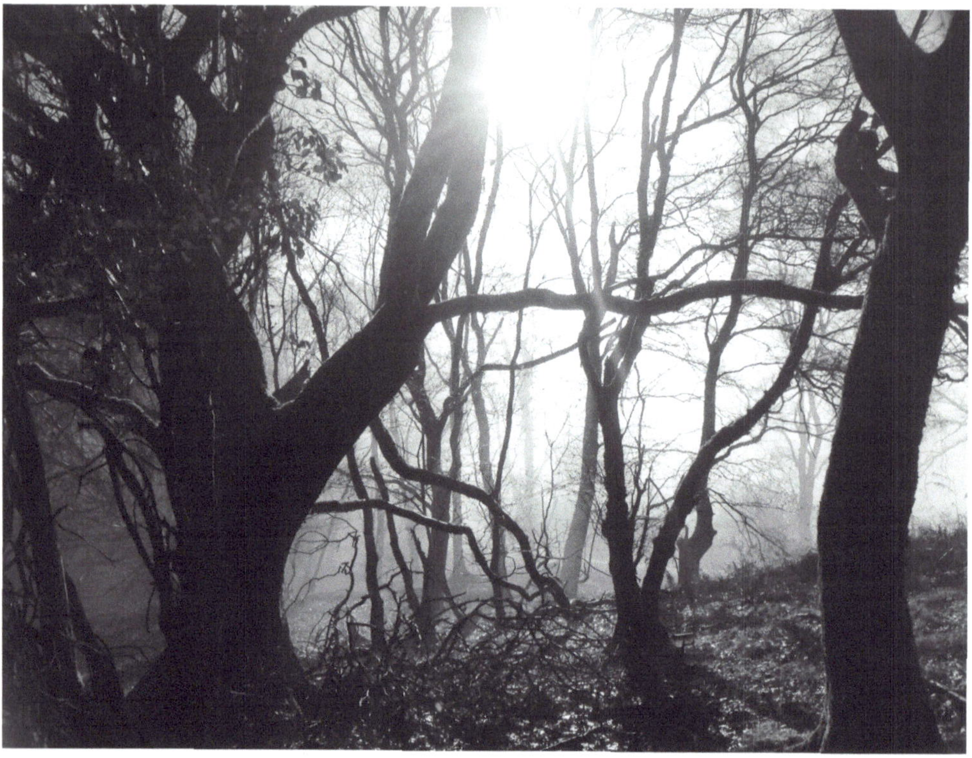

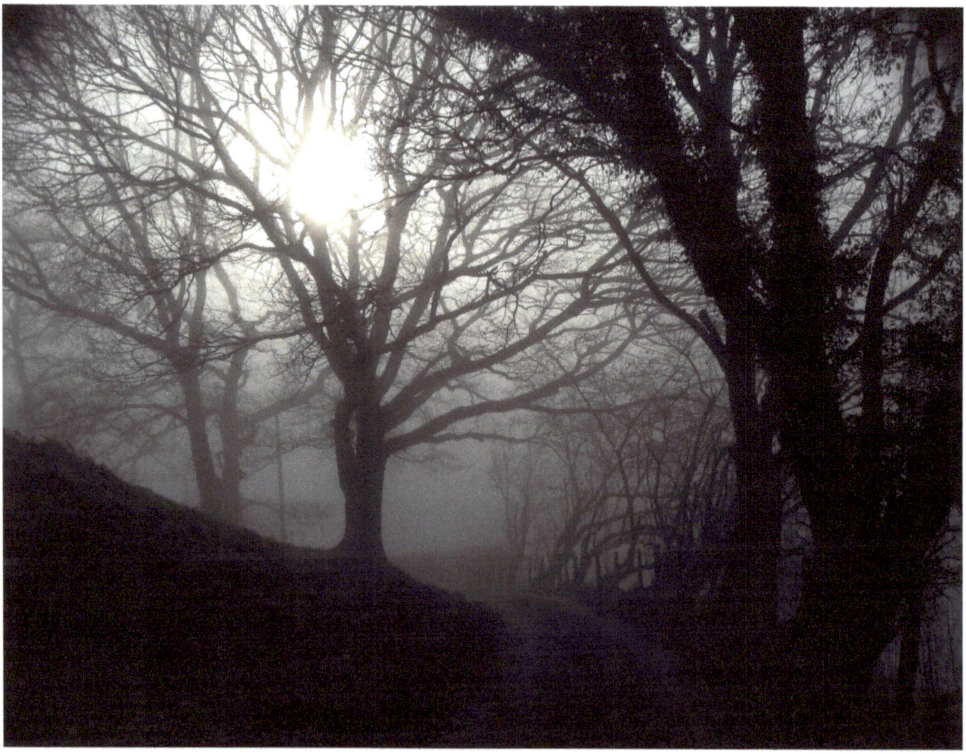

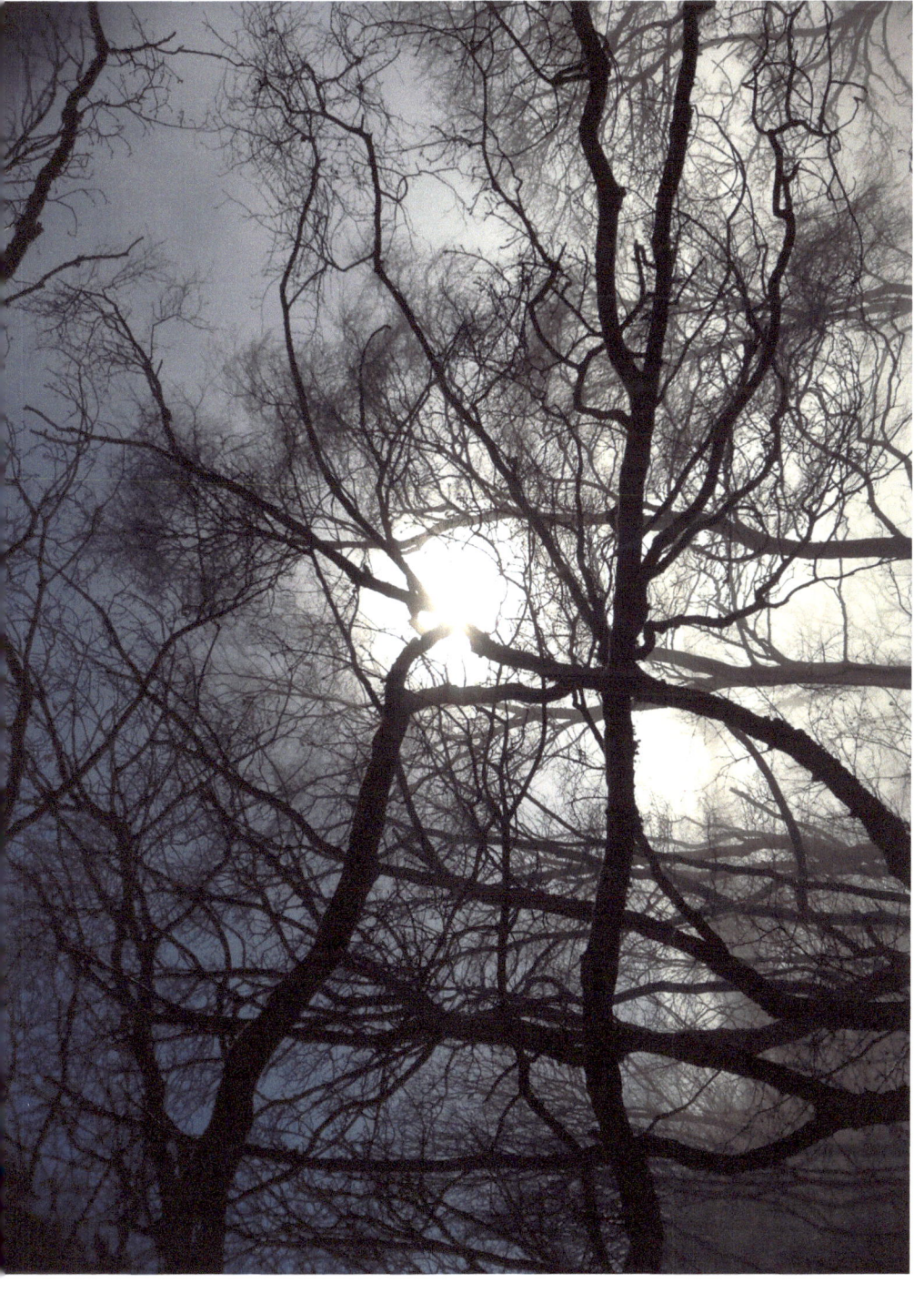

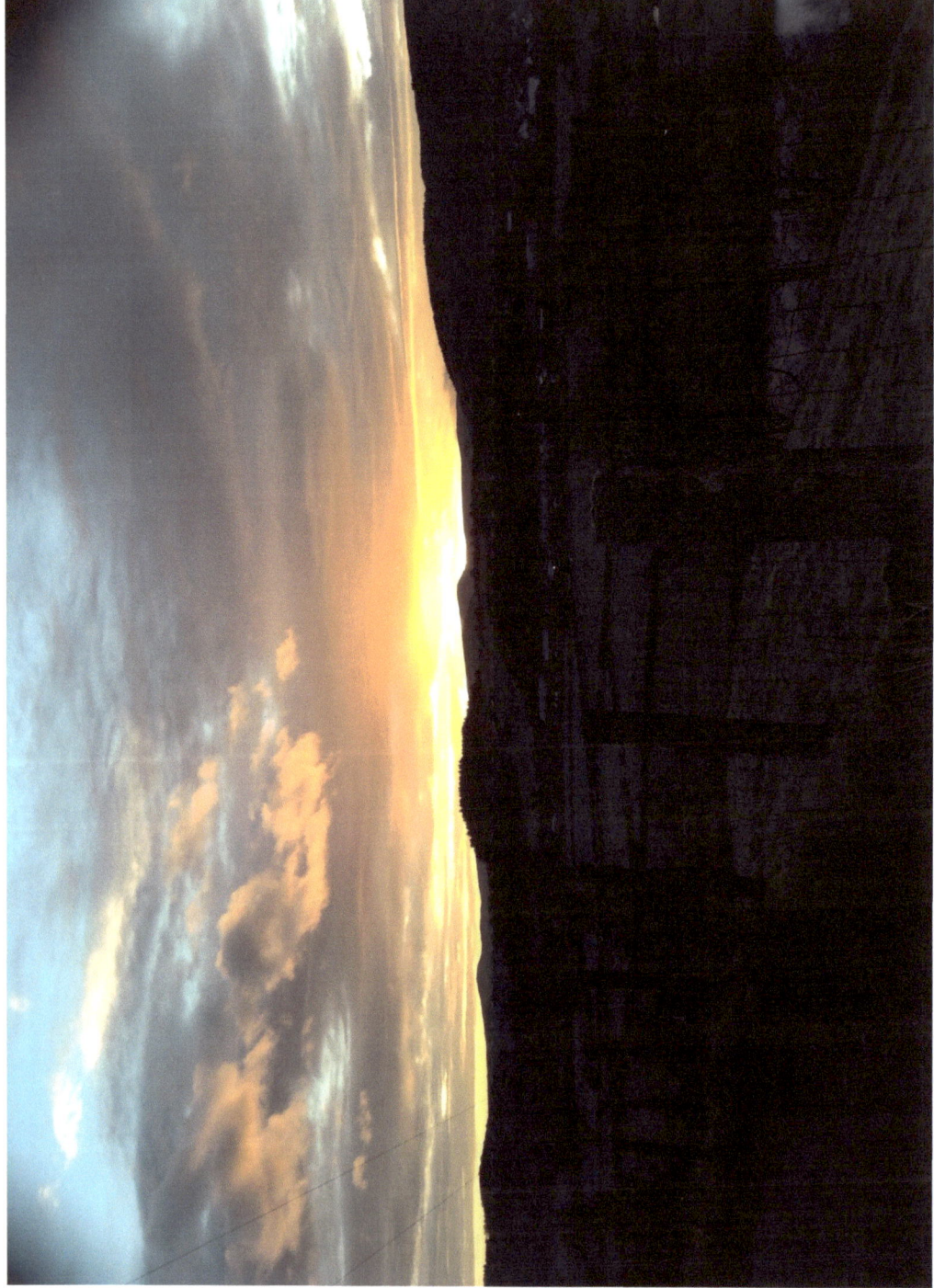

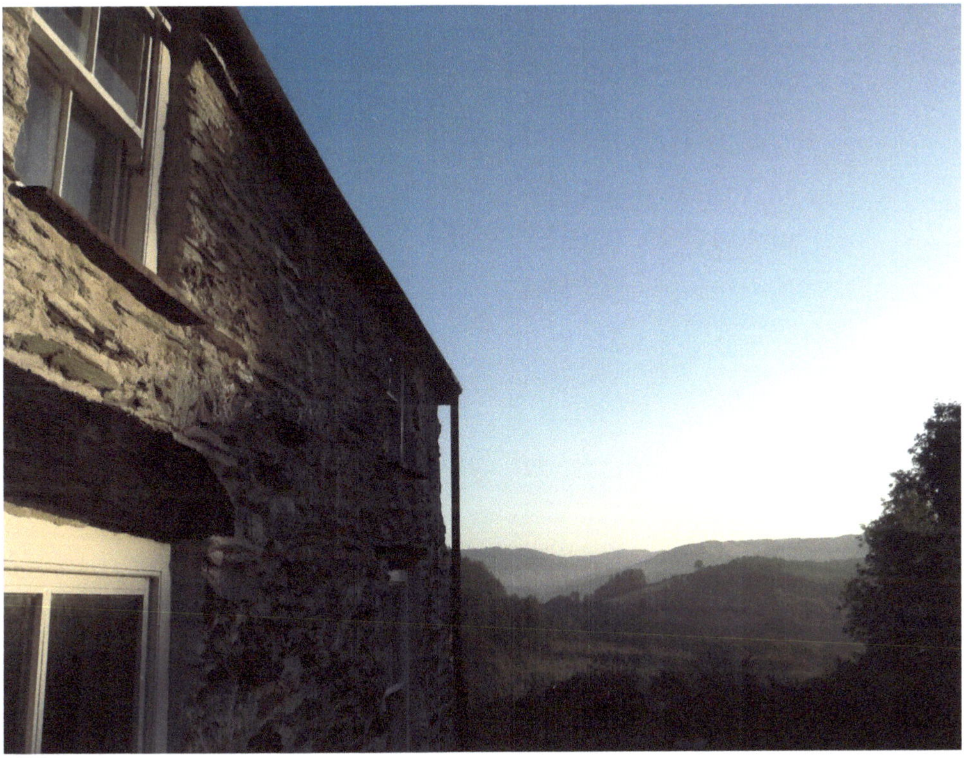

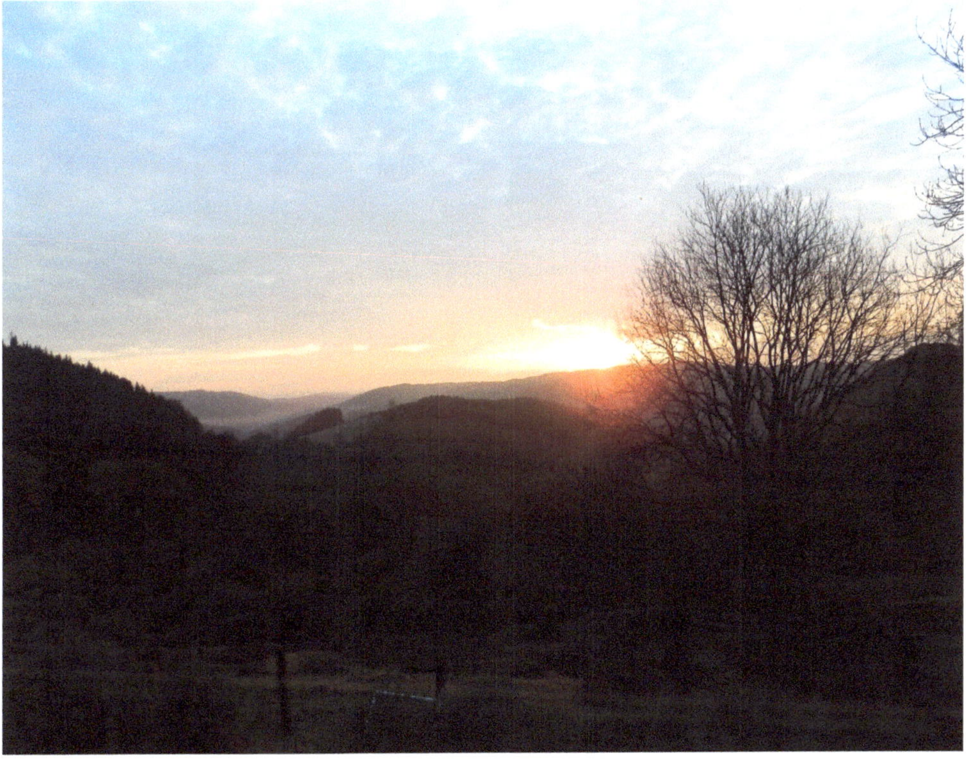

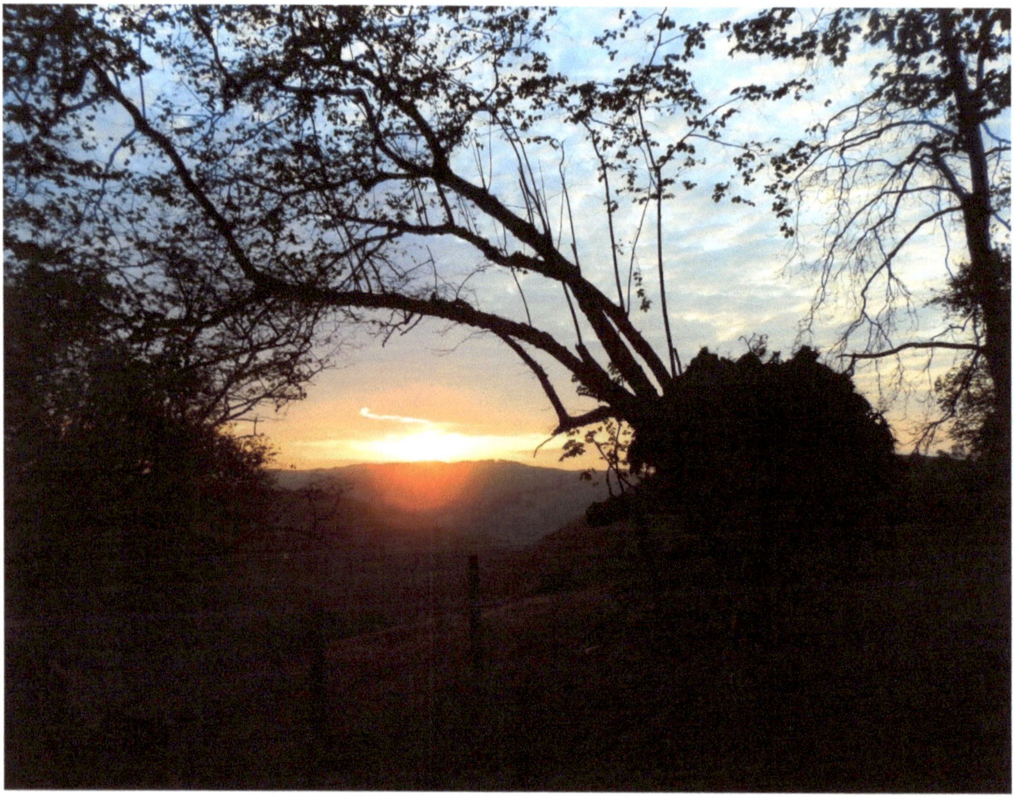

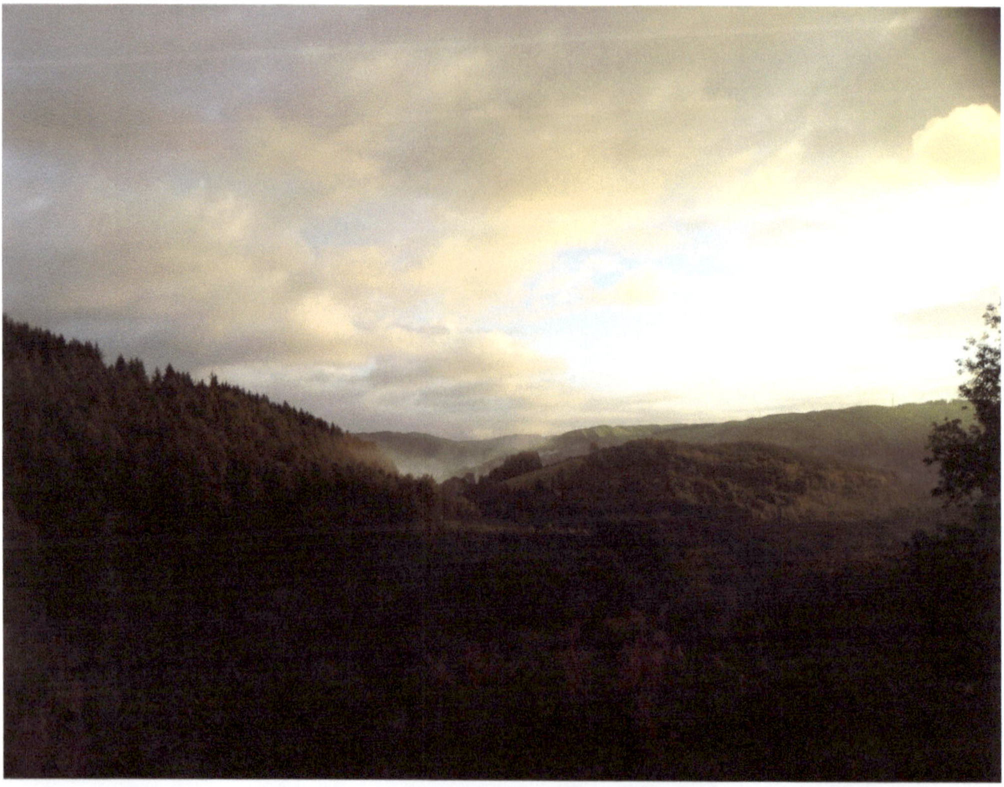

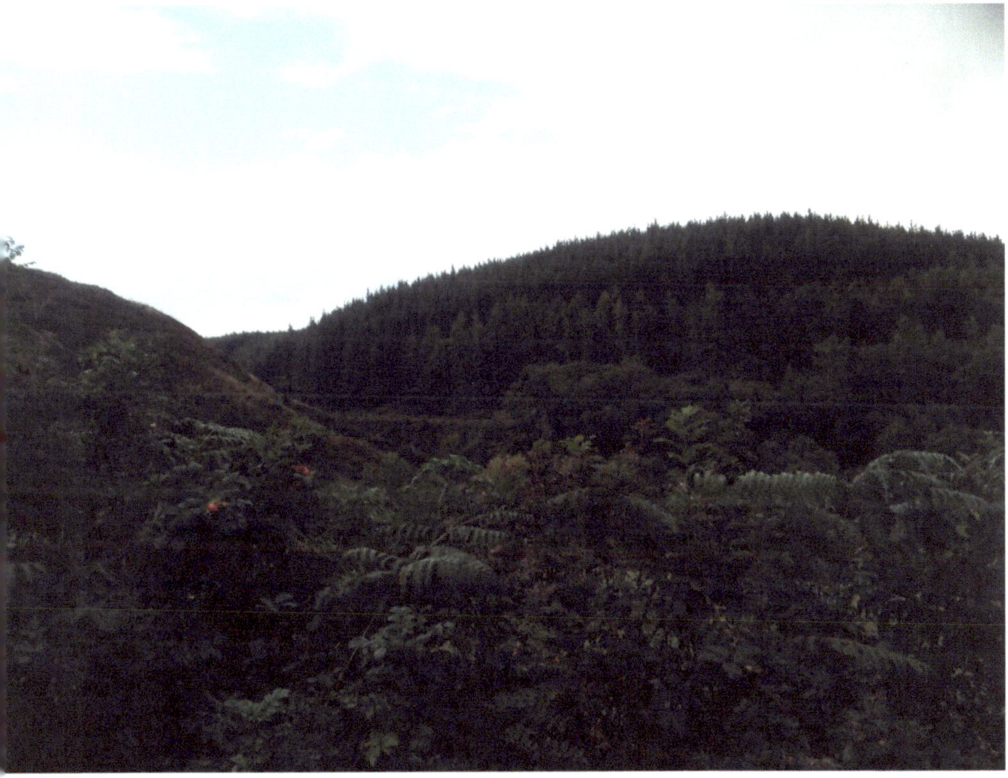

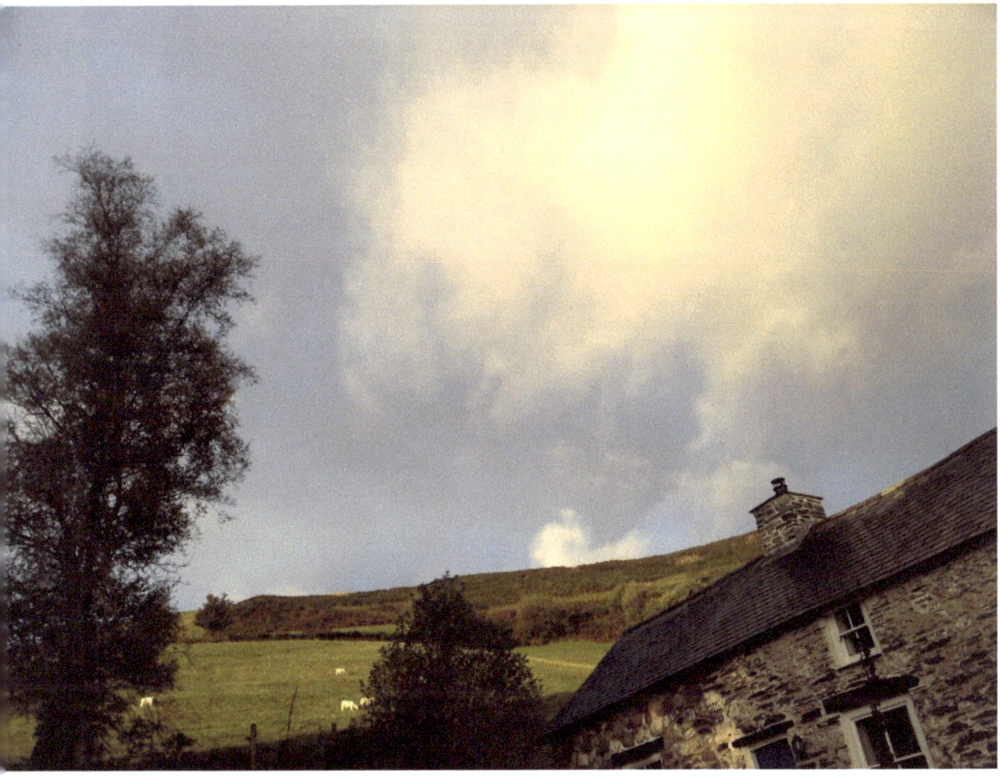

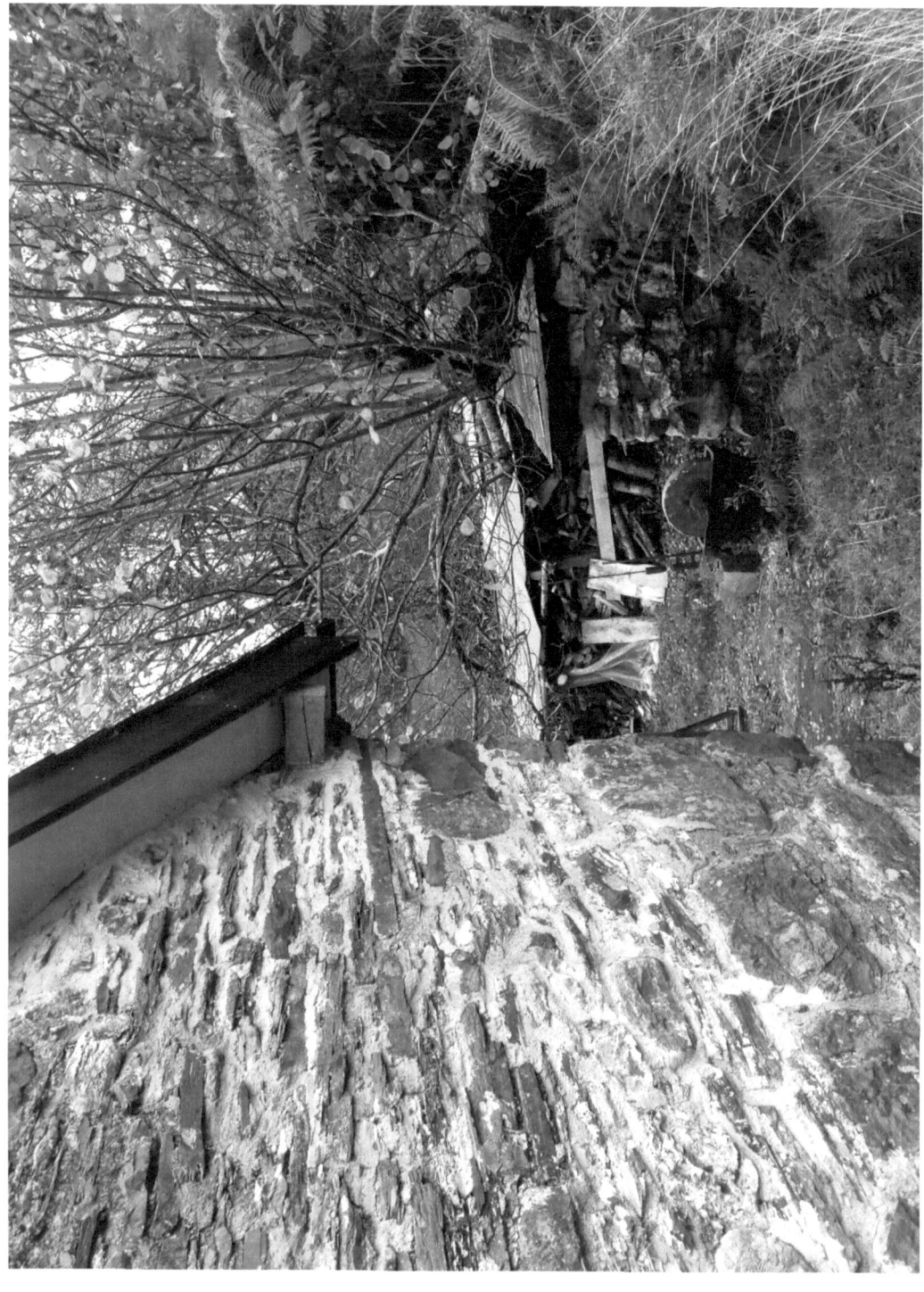

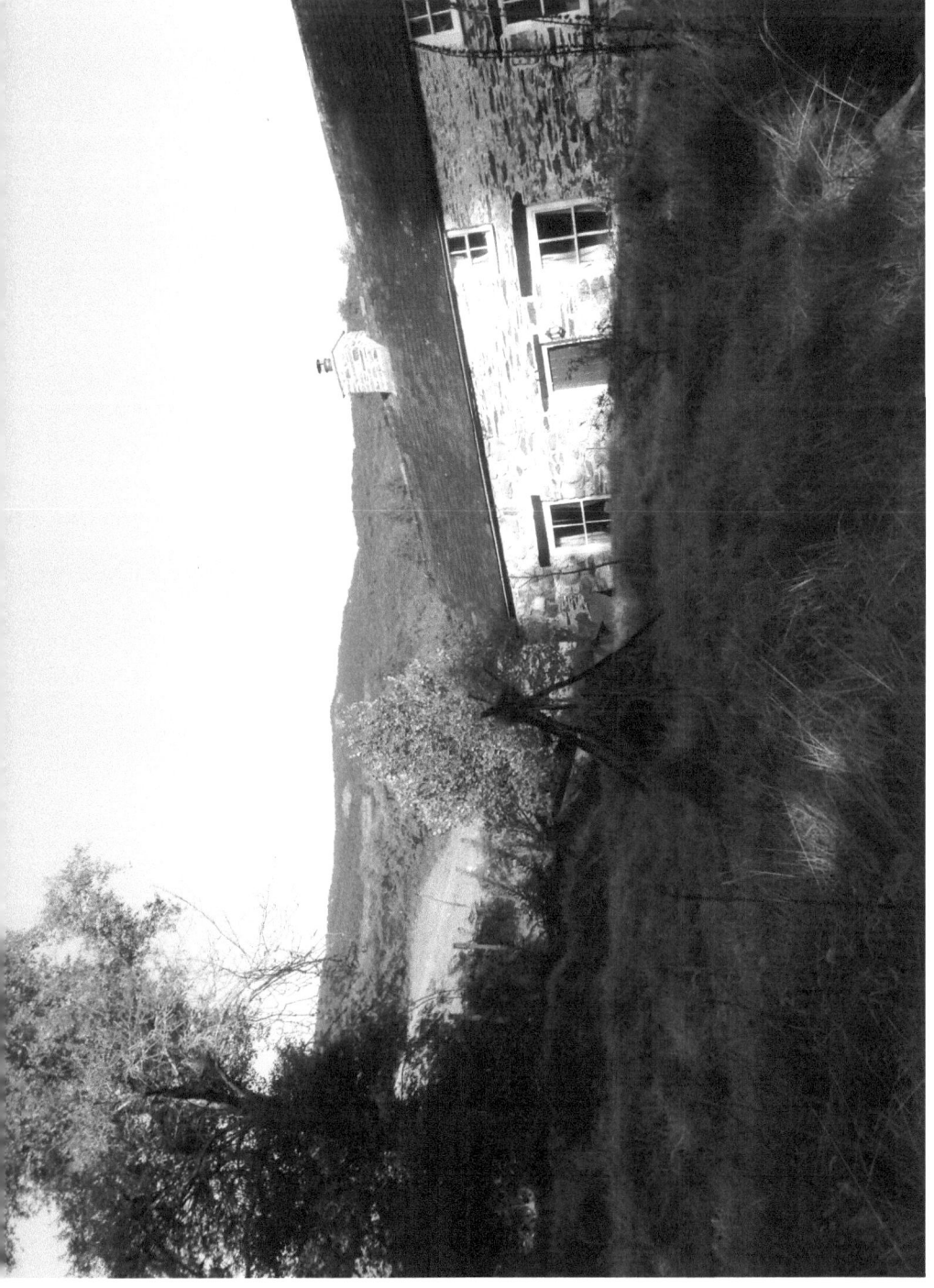